What God Reads in His Spare Time

To Carol,

Thanks for your support. Thanks for coming to the signing. I have fond memories of you and SMS. Best always.

What God Reads in His Spare Time

—⋙—

A. B. (Barney) Sloan

A. G. Sloan

ISBN-13: 9781511864855
ISBN-10: 1511864850
Library of Congress Control Number: 2015906848
CreateSpace Independent Publishing Platform,
North Charleston, SC

Dedication

To my wife Pixie, if I had half the faith in myself that she has in me, I would be the king of the world, and she would be the queen instead of just my princess.

Table of Contents

Acknowledgments

As of this writing, the following articles from this book have appeared in *Funny Times*:

"O Come Back All Ye Faithful," April 2013

"Death Be a Lot Proud," July 2013

"Talkin' 'Bout my Generation," October 2013

"The Long and Binding Road," March 2014

"They're Playing our Son," May 2014

"Minority Opinion," November 2014

"What to Expect in the Sixty-Fifth Year, Chapter 4, The Male Retiree," February 2015.

"Deadline," July 2015

I'd like to thank the following people:

My father, who was funny but not nearly as funny as he thought he was.

My mother, who is funny but mostly unintentionally.

My sister Betty, who is funny (see father comment), thus making me the fourth funniest in the family.

My wife Pixie; we are the greatest love story ever told.

My sons Damon and Daniel, who usually laugh at my jokes and will continue to do so if they know what's good for them.

My daughters-in-law Mariah and Ana, who always support my work.

My grandchildren Elena, Braden, Riley, Philip, and Warren, just because you're you. By the way, you are not allowed to read this book until I'm gone, and I don't mean when I'm out of town.

All my other family members, I hope something in this book makes you laugh.

My nearly 4,000 former junior high students who endured my comments, but I'm sure the ones who laughed have gone on to do great things.

My former colleagues, who had to listen to me in the lunchroom and at faculty meetings, but I'm sure those of you who laughed have gone on to do great things.

My friends, who must be weary of my constant interjections of one-liners during our conversations. I know I'm annoying, but I don't think I can stop.

Sandee and Ray at *Funny Times* for publishing my work so I have an outlet for my craziness.

Sister Clementine who, when I was in eighth grade, slapped me across the face. You made me the man I am today.

Bob, Jim, and Charlie who, with me, wrote the first "What God Reads in His Spare Time."

Everyone else I've ever met who helped me find the funny in almost every situation.

Foreword

First of all, I want to apologize to anyone and everyone who might be offended by something or some things in this book. It is in vogue for people to be easily offended (I hope that doesn't offend you) and even more in vogue for people to apologize. Therefore, I am sorry for whatever it might be I have to be sorry for. I hope you accept my apology, because I wouldn't want us to get off on the wrong foot (not that I want to get off on your foot) and prevent you from enjoying the parts of this book that do not offend you. I also hope that this apology has come across as sincere, because I wouldn't want you to think that I'm simply blowing smoke to get you to think I'm nice when I'm really an insensitive jerk.

They say the first rule for a writer is to write what you know, but I didn't think a blank book was a very good idea. So I decided that the only way to fill enough for a book was to make up stuff. Although, that blank book idea is intriguing. I would call it *The Author Doesn't Know Anything, so This Book Is Blank*. I would love for a copy to be in my library. I would scout out the section and watch people. How many people would be able to just look at the title and put it back? How many people would flip through the pages quickly? How many people would go through it, page by page, thinking—like someone watching an Andy Warhol movie—that there must be something else to this? And I'd really like to have a discussion with the person who decides to check it out. Very existential, don't you think?

Admittedly, my writing experience has been limited. In college, three other guys and I wrote a book together. One person would write a page but leave his last sentence at the top of the next page. Then the next person would go in and try to resume the story, and so on. We found it entertaining, but it was mostly crap until we decided to actually work on it. We gave it to two of our English professors, and they gave us honest feedback, some of it good, some of it scathing.

The book, by the way, was called *What God Reads in His Spare Time*. We only had one copy. We lent it out to someone, who lent it to someone else, and on and on until we lost track of it and never got it back. Maybe this book should be considered a sequel and should be called *What God Reads in His Spare Time, Again*. I hope the title attracts people to the book and that I'm not sorry I didn't use the other title I had in mind, which was *Greasing the Slide to Hell*.

Since then I have dabbled in a few attempts at writing. I wrote a short story called "Moveable Prison" that I entered in a *Writer's Digest* magazine contest. Out of about three thousand entries, the story ranked number sixty-two. I wrote a couple of humor articles that were published in the *Chicago Tribune* and in a local newspaper. I even tried writing joke ideas and captions for cartoonists. I sold two. One of them was based on a commercial. A man looks into the camera and says, "I want to talk to you about diarrhea." For my joke, I simply added, "but I really have to run." The other one was a bit risqué. There are three prostitutes on the corner, and the third one is holding a sign that says "Express Lane." The magazine that the cartoonist sold it to was even dirtier than the joke.

During that time I wrote a story called "Our Father." It was greatly influenced by Kurt Vonnegut because I was reading all of his work at the time. I decided to write him a fan letter and tell him about the story, which was my attempt to be funny and touching while at the same time being science fictiony, a la Vonnegut. This was his response:

"That's a good story you tell in your letter, and you could have sold it to twenty different publications back in the golden age of magazines. What can I say? Things are a lot tougher all around than they were when I was a kid. Really.

Cheers-----

Kurt Vonnegut"

After "Cheers" there was a handwritten, practically indecipherable signature.

I never sold that story, and I didn't write much after that. In the summer of 2012, I was in the hospital for five days. There's no better place to mull over what you want to do with the rest of your life. My first idea was to travel neighborhoods across the country pressing my garage door opener to see if anyone else was on my frequency, but that seemed like a lot of driving. So I decided I wanted to write and get published. The first piece that was accepted is the first one in this book. It first appeared in *Funny Times*. As indicated in the acknowledgments, they have already published a number of these articles.

This led to my second fan letter. Another writer whose work I admire is Dave Barry. His work also appears in *Funny Times*. I wrote him to tell him of my admiration, and to say I was proud to have my work in the same publication as his. He wrote back:

"Thanks. I wish you luck.

Your fellow columnist--

(Signed) Dave Barry"

There are forty articles in this book. I stopped there because forty is a significant number: forty winks, forty days and nights of the great flood, Lizzie Borden's number of axe whacks, and the last age that made any sense to me.

Finally, I tried to get Michael Moore to write this foreword. He is my neighbor after all. But he didn't think it would be right for him to do it because he's not much of a writer, and he's a dentist. It was worth a shot.

Death Be a Lot Proud

When I was young, I worried about everything: acne, sex, dating, sex, marriage, sex, kids, sex, job, sex, money, and sex. One of the perks of getting old(er) is that all of these, including, believe it or not, sex, are overshadowed by one simple worry: DEATH.

My goal has always been to never experience death, but, from what I can gather from the Internet, it is inevitable. If there ever were any immortal people, I'm sure they're dead by now. Accepting that, I now want to make sure it happens in the right way. I can accept death more readily if it is not what I consider a stupid demise.

I can deal with the two biggest killers: heart disease and cancer. There's something noble and very American about dying by one of those methods. "Hey, so I heard Barney died. What happened?"

"Oh, man, he had a MASSIVE HEART ATTACK." Or, "Poor guy went after a long, COURAGEOUS BATTLE WITH CANCER." There are two ways, however, that would fall into the stupid demise category, so now I divide every year into two seasons: flu and West Nile Virus. No offense to any of you who have died from, or lost a loved one to, one of these two conditions, but they're just not for me.

The flu is something you're supposed to have for a while and get over. "Fred, where you been all week?"

"Oh, man, I had the worst case of the flu. Fever, aches, vomiting. Just horrible."

That's what the conversation should be, not, "Where's Fred been this week?"

"He had the flu."

"That's too bad. When's he coming back to work?

"He's not."

It's even worse for the West Nile Virus. "Bates died, huh?"

"Yeah, sad."

"Was it a MASSIVE HEART ATTACK or a LONG BATTLE WITH CANCER?"

"Nope, mosquito."

All year round, my energies are directed at the prevention of these maladies. During flu season, from October to April, I have no contact with anyone unless it's absolutely necessary, and necessary means an emergency. And an emergency means you better be freakin' dying before you call me, and even then you should be calling 911 and leaving me out of your problems. No lunch dates with friends, no babysitting runny-nosed, hack-coughing grandkids, no grocery shopping trips that force me to touch those diseased shopping carts. If my wife so much as asks me if it's warm in the house or is it her, I retreat to my man bedroom (no cave) to sleep and watch TV. For the other five months of the year, I live more normally, except that no matter where I go or what the weather, I wear a hooded sweatshirt, long pants, socks, and steel-toed boots. I am also always drenched with Deep Woods Off. I sleep this way too.

But it's not enough to simply prevent these conditions. I must also be proactive to bring on at least one of the big two. As a result, I have adopted many new behaviors. I do not exercise, I drink hard liquor and smoke three packs of cigarettes a day, volunteer to do asbestos removal, eat nothing but red meat cooked on a charcoal grill, drink bottled water *and* tap water, drink diet soda *and* regular soda, stand naked in front of an operating microwave, tell the dentist not to put the lead vest on me during X-rays, and I roll around on my lawn immediately after the weed control company sprays poison on my grass. In between all of this, I try to have as much strenuous sex as possible.

I really hope all of my efforts lead to a happy ending.

Seen but Not Heard

Are you embarrassed when you read newspaper articles about how American students are stupid? Are you tired of hearing that, when asked in what decade the Civil War occurred, our students say, "What's a decade?" Are you sickened to learn they can't locate Canada on a map of Canada? We all are.

The politicians and experts have all weighed in on how to repair our educational system. Some want to fund it more, some think teachers should be held more accountable, some believe students should be tested every eighteen minutes even outside of school hours.

I am here to tell you that these, and all of the many other ideas they may concoct, stink. The only way to improve education is to return to the GOLDEN AGE of EDUCATION, (unsure of exact dates), and exert more pressure on kids to work hard and behave properly. I have an invention that will do just that and revolutionize the entire educational system. It is guaranteed to ensure that all students will put forth their best effort and achieve their maximum potential.

The answer to all of the ills of education is replacing traditional student desks with soundproof booths. Because I am the inventor, we'll call them Sloan Booths. If you're old enough, you might remember the ones that were used in the old rigged quiz shows. Mine are similar but tweaked for educational purposes. Each Sloan Booth is equipped with a desk, chair, speakers, microphone, a pneumatic tube for turning in homework, and a closed-circuit TV monitor.

They are constructed of see-through, reinforced glass in the front (on second thought, better add bulletproof), and solid steel on the other three sides, so students see only in front of them. The monitor allows them to see the teacher just in case their view is obstructed by other booths.

The design itself remedies many of the minor infractions that happen in classrooms across this country every day. Immediately there can be no note passing, no spit wad throwing, no feet putting on the desk in front, no pigtail pulling, nothing.

But wait. There's more. In addition, the teacher has access to a control panel at his or her desk to operate all of the handy features of the booths. Each cubicle is wired for sound. Controlling sound is one of the most important aspects of a teacher's day. What's the most common of the minor infractions that a teacher faces every day? Talking. A problem, but now a thing of the past with the Sloan Booth.

During a teacher's lecture, the speakers are turned on in the students' booths, but the students' microphones are off. Nobody hears anyone except the teacher. During class discussions, all sound and microphones are opened; however, if a student talks out of turn, the teacher can simply shut off that student's microphone. The student now will hear everything but can no longer participate.

OK, we've taken care of the classroom management problems. What can the Sloan Booth do for academics? The answer is everything. Doing the work and paying attention are the keys to academic success. The Sloan Booth guarantees that students will do both. Academics and discipline are closely tied because sometimes students need a little prodding to work and pay attention. To that end, the Sloan Booth gives teachers access to the tools that encourage the students: temperature control, air supply, and electrification.

Let's look at some examples of how a teacher might use these features. If a student doesn't turn in a homework assignment, the teacher might cut the oxygen in the booth for a time while asking, "You'll remember your homework tomorrow, won't you? Won't you?" Chances are the student will soon answer in the affirmative and not miss another assignment.

Maybe a student falls asleep during a teacher's lecture. No need to walk over to the booth and knock. Simply go to the control panel and give the sleepy urchin a little jolt. He will forever be bright-eyed and bushy-tailed from then on.

These fun controls and how they are used would be left to the discretion of the teacher. Eventually the teacher will know what works for each student: when to turn up the heat, when to freeze them out, when to turn off the air, and when to give them the juice.

After these booths are in every classroom in America, we will no longer be the laughingstock of every other industrialized nation, and we will return to our rightful place as the smartest people in the world. With the Sloan Booth, truly no child will be left behind even though his or her behind might be a little charred.

Walk Three Miles in My Shoes

I walk three miles almost every day. I don't say that to brag because most people my age can do it. It's just that their attitude is, "What the hell's the point?" They're probably right. I'm walking for forty minutes every day to add maybe 1.7 years to my lifespan. Isn't it better to live my forty minutes when I'm younger than living another 1.7 years when I'm near the end anyway? Not only that, but there are a few other reasons that venturing out on the neighborhood trek might be more trouble and more dangerous than it should be.

It seems everyone on my route has at least one dog. Don't get me wrong. I like dogs. Really I do. Honest. But I take the expression once bitten twice shy literally, because a few summers ago I was bitten by a dog. The dog was with its owner and on a leash, and it still managed to take a chunk from the back of my calf. The owner apologized and said the dog had never bitten anyone before. I not so cheerfully responded that he'd never be able to say that again as I dabbed blood from my leg.

The scariest moments come from the dogs that are kept in their yards by an invisible fence. I still don't trust the dogs or the fences. Every day I am met by a dog that charges toward me from his hiding place. He travels the perimeter of his yard, following me while barking and looking directly at me. I can tell what he's thinking: "One of these days, I'm not going to give a shit about a little shock, and I'm coming to get you, you bastard."

Oftentimes, there are groups of kids as well. Don't get me wrong. I like kids. Really I do. Honest. But I don't like to come across a group of them while I'm walking. Sometimes I start to run when I see a group, but even then I get the feeling they're talking about me. "Look at that really old guy running," they whisper incredulously. They all stop and stare at me, like NASCAR fans waiting for the big crash.

The worst is if they are playing hoops in a driveway. Inevitably, the ball bounces away from them and in my direction. They don't want me to just toss it back. They taunt me to take a shot in a tone of voice that means, "Let's see what you got old man." Well, I got nothing. I couldn't shoot a basketball when I was eighteen, never mind when I'm…now. More than likely I will either clank it off the rim or, worse yet, throw up an air ball. The kids will say, "Oh, too bad, "while thinking, "You suck."

Then there are other walkers. Don't get me wrong. I like other people. Really I do. Honest. But I don't like them around me while I'm walking. The worst are the people who are walking behind me at about the same pace and going exactly where I'm going. It doesn't matter if it's a man or woman. I am intimidated. Nobody can tell by looking at me (or maybe they can) that I have the strength of many gnats. Even the aforementioned kids could take me down. Thankfully, they aren't aware of that.

I live in a very safe neighborhood, but when you're paranoid like I am, you can never be sure. Maybe I'd feel better if I had a dog with me.

Grandkids, Glasses, Television...

Ever since I was blessed with grandchildren, I've had to sit through watching kids' shows. It's my own fault. I let television do my baby-sitting. Those of you who play educational games, read, and do arts and crafts projects with kids, go ahead and feel superior. I don't care. Judge me all you want. I'm old and tired.

But I am paying the price because it is excruciating to watch what they like. All of the shows have one thing in common, monotony. There are usually two characters, or sometimes an entire team of characters, that have some problem to solve or some destination to reach. For example, Dora and Boots might have to get to Ice Cream Castle, but first they must cross the River of Piranhas and go through the Forest of Zombies. Over and over again, they will repeat where they have been and where they still need to go.

"Where are we going? Piranhas, zombies, Ice Cream Castle. Say it with us: piranhas, zombies, Ice Cream Castle. We made it over the River of Piranhas. Where do we need to go next? The Forest of Zombies, right!"

They're always yelling at the kids and making them say things and repeat them over and over and over. Shut up already. You're giving me a headache. I secretly wish they will fall in the river, ending the episode and maybe the series.

Or the Paw Patrol or Team Umizoomi has a problem to solve. This is an actual dilemma from one program: "Anthony has lost his package. We need your help to find Anthony's package. Will you help us find Anthony's package? Great! We know that Anthony's package is red and heart-shaped. When you see a red, heart-shaped package, yell package!"

"*Package!*"

"Now we have to mail Anthony's package. First of all, we need to weigh Anthony's package. How much does his package weigh? Seven units, right! Based on the weight of Anthony's package, how many stamps do we need to mail Anthony's package? Eight, that's right!" I would have loved to have been in the writers' room when they churned out that one.

What's worse is that kids don't watch each episode once. They have to watch it every day, even multiple times in a day. "We want to see the zombie Dora one," they demand. "We want to watch Anthony's package again." So the headache continues.

But my biggest aversion to these shows is that they mirror my own life. That's right, my life has become a kids' show. For example, I will tell my wife I'm going to run a few errands, and she will say, "Could you also drop this book off at the library and go buy some stamps?"

I picture the order in which I need to do these stops: library, bank, post office, pharmacy, gas station. Library, bank, post office, pharmacy, gas station. Where am I going? Say it with me: library, bank, post office, pharmacy, gas station.

Then there is the real life search for my glasses. When this happens and the grandkids are there, I use the shows' techniques to help me. "Grandpa has lost his glasses," I announce to my charges. "Will you help me find them?" They, I think reluctantly, agree to the game. "Let's think of some places where Grandpa may have lost them. Let's try all the surfaces in the house where he might have set them down, but he has no recollection of where. Are they on a dresser, a kitchen counter, the end table, in the bed?" No, they are not in any of those places.

At this point, I realize the team needs a break. "We'll get back to the mysterious disappearance of Grandpa's glasses, but right now does anybody know what time it is?"

"*Snack time!*"

"Yes, it is! Go to the kitchen and get what you'd like."

I continue to search unsuccessfully for the glasses while I check on baby Warren. Soon I return to the kitchen to check on snack time. Riley has microwaved popcorn. Braden has potato chips. Elena has goldfish crackers, and Philip has Twizzlers. But they are more excited about something else. They run to me as they blurt out words that eventually mean, "Grandpa, we went to the refrigerator for some peach mango juice, and on the top shelf we found your glasses!"

"Thanks, Team Grandkids."

Who says television isn't educational?

Living on a Prayer

Even people with absolutely no skills of perception can take one look at me and think I have a sexual problem. Those people would be right.

I am a Catholic school survivor from the '60s. Many readers are probably thinking that I could stop there, and they would understand my situation. Those people would be wrong. Although I was an altar boy from fourth grade to college, I was never approached by a priest. Most of the ones I knew were womanizing alcoholics. Over the years, as I have heard about the church's scandal, I admit that, although I am happy not to have been a victim, the neglect may have damaged some of my self-esteem. Like, hey, you guys, what was wrong with me? But that is not the cause of my sexual malady.

The root of it goes back to early grade school when every hour on the hour we had to ejaculate. That's right. From nine to three every day for eight years, a little bell would ring, and Sister Mary Muhammad Ali would say that it was time for our ejaculation. We would then all say in unison, if we knew what was good for us, "Jesus, Mary, and Joseph, pray for us." For those eight years, that was the only definition of that word that I ever knew: a short emotional utterance or a prayer.

Even though I went to Catholic school, I had a few friends who were publics, that is, public school attendees. The publics seemed to be less sheltered than us privates. Anything sexual would first be brought up by a public. We privates usually just listened, laughed, and pretended to know what they were talking about. One day, when

I was almost thirteen, I was alone with my friend Terry, a public, and he started in on me.

He elbowed me with a sly smile on his face and asked, "Have you ever ejaculated?"

I was surprised to hear a public use the word. He couldn't possibly know about this. They didn't pray in public school. I looked at him suspiciously. "Yeah, a lot."

"A lot, huh," he said incredulously. "Isn't it great?"

"Uh, it's OK, I guess. No big deal. After so many times, it gets a little boring."

"Boring? You're an idiot, Sloan. Something must be wrong with you because it's the greatest thing I've ever experienced, especially when I wake up in the middle of the night and enjoy it. That ever happen to you?"

"No, I'm a pretty good sleeper. An occasional trip to the bathroom, but that's all."

This went on for a while with my friend just shaking his head and calling me names, and neither of us figuring out that we were not on the same talking point. A short time later, toward the end of eighth grade, our parish priest came to our classroom to speak to the boys. The girls were taken out of our classroom by (anachronism alert!) Sister Mary Mike Tyson and sequestered in some undisclosed location for the rest of the day. Surprisingly, it was sex talk day.

I don't remember a great deal about the content of the day. I'm sure it was sketchy at best. But I do remember hearing about wet dreams and the word ejaculate and finding out that it had another totally different meaning. The sound of my hand slapping my forehead was loud enough for everyone, including the priest, to stop and turn toward me. I tried to make it look like there was a bug flying around as I was screaming inside, "So that's what Terry was talking about!"

So what is my problem? To this day, I cannot complete the sex act without yelling, "Jesus, Mary, and Joseph, pray for us."

What's in a Name?

I think people should be more careful when naming their children, because I believe that what they choose actually affects who and what those children become. Sure, genetics and environment are important, but a name determines a person's behavior, occupation, interests, indeed, their entire personality.

It seems that people want to go off the board when choosing the monikers of their offspring. Celebrities are particularly notorious for this trend. Consider this short list of names: Blue Ivy, Apple, Tripp, Blanket, and Pilot Inspektor. Kids with names like these can only turn out one way—weird.

Do you really want to take a chance with these goofy names for your child? Go ahead. Name your next kid Crackhead and see how he develops. You will have virtually no control over his destiny, and you will be blamed for it all simply because you made a poor choice of a name.

But even the more popular and regular names should not be taken lightly. The usual "baby book" names already carry with them preconceptions of whom the persons will be. A few examples: Ryans are brats, Genes are stupid, Marks are intelligent, and Arnolds go to *Star Trek* conventions. Jennifers are quiet, Michelles are cheerleaders, Dawns are spacy, Tammys are sexy, and Zeldas are crazy. Tell me your kid's name, and I'll tell you who they are.

If you're still not convinced, then explain why the neighborhood bully is always named Tony, Rick, or Mike instead of Dennis, Bruce, or Herbert. While the former group terrorizes neighborhoods, the latter group busies itself by reading Proust and practicing the cello.

How many Harvard professors are named Rocky? How many boxers are named Irwin?

However, what you name your kid may not be as important as what you call him or her. For example, if you name your son William and call him William, he's likely to become a writer or a network president. If you call him Bill, he'll be a carpenter or a truck driver. Call him Billy and add his middle name, and now you've got a country singer or a mass murderer, or perhaps both. This theory gets so specific that I even heard of a family whose children were each named after a different criminal, and all of them had been in trouble with the law.

Of course, prejudice, even name prejudice, can be dangerous. During the fall when I was a kid, my friends and I played pickup football games every Sunday. One time, one of the players brought two of his cousins, Frank and Clarence. Frank was a big, burly, squatty lineman type. Clarence was the tall, skinny, bespectacled, bookworm type.

My team had first pick and we took Frank. Clarence, as we learned after the game, was a wide receiver for his freshman high school football team. Frank, as it turned out, could barely walk. We lost 115–0.

Oh, by the way, the initials A. G. in my name stand for Authoring Greatness.

3out My Generation

...ose of us born between 1946–1964, are a
...ed someone to advocate for us. I don't mean
...or Social Security and health issues. We need
...s in a positive light because, I believe, we are
...re by a number of negative stereotypes. The
...s us as stupid, old, drugged-out, free-loving,
...en hippies who have turned into disgruntled

Until an organization can be formed, however, I will be the group's self-appointed, unofficial spokesperson. Where to begin! Let's address the curmudgeon accusation first because there is some truth to it. Are we crabby a lot? Yes, but with good reason. We are the generation that has adult children, grandchildren, and/or our parents living with us. And usually we're the only one in the house-hold with a job. Tell me that you wouldn't turn into a sourpuss with all those people hanging around.

We are accused of just saying whatever we think in every situation. We may be outspoken, but not nearly as much as we'd like. Believe it or not, we have a filter. We have kids, grandkids, in-laws, friends, neighbors, and hired help. There simply is not enough time in the day to tell off all those people. We are actually being selective.

One of the most prevalent stereotypes is that we are stupid. All right, maybe we can't install a car seat, or take one out, or put a kid in one, or get a kid out of one, but that's no way to measure our relative intelligence. Remember that horde of people living with us? These are the people who think we don't know anything. I know this because none of them ever listen to what we tell them. More than likely, if they did, our houses would have fewer inhabitants.

Our parents were part of the Greatest Generation, but the Boomers have done better than them. Maybe we should be called the Better than the Greatest Generation Generation. In addition, our children are part of the generation that will be the first known one that will not do better than the previous one. So, we surpassed the previous generation, and the next one has not measured up. How stupid can we be?

Our stupidity supposedly extends to technology. Presumably, we are unable to deal with computers, smartphones, iPads, and so forth. Who do you think is buying these newfangled inventions that update more often than the Stock Market ticker? We're the only people who have any money. We're buying them and using them. If anyone from another generation has any of these things, it's because a Boomer bought it for him.

In addition, who are the big names in technology? Bill Gates, Paul Allen, and Steve Jobs. Booyah, all Boomers. Because of them, our generation brought computers into the workplace and ultimately into our homes. These were the early machines that worked about 30 percent of the time. We were the ones who showed our kids how to insert a floppy disk and play Breakout and Pitfall on a Commodore 64. We were the ones who learned to surf the Internet when there were only three websites, and at any given time two of them were down.

Most of our government leaders belong to the Baby Boomer generation. We are basically running the country. As a result, our so-called hippie-like tendencies concerning pot and sex have infiltrated society, and oh, what they have wrought! Look at how quickly medical marijuana is becoming legal. Even recreational use has begun its journey to legalization. To the younger generations, you're welcome.

Also, because of the aging of the Boomers, something had to be done about erectile dysfunction. The sexual revolution pioneers were not going down easily. No pun intended. Many generations to come, again no pun intended, will look at the history of weed and E. D. meds and thank us.

Advocating for such a large group that needs so much damage control has taken a lot out of me. So, if you don't mind, I'm going to make my mother some tea, read a story to my granddaughter, talk to my son about looking for work, take my "medication," and go to bed.

Celebrity Makeover

In the poetic, immortal words of both rock and roll band The Cars and a Disney Channel show, I need to "shake it up." Everything about my appearance is bland, boring, and predictable. I need something or some things that will make people take notice and say, "Hey, that's new. That's different. That's awesome."

Clothes

I wear, and have worn for the last thirty years, the same kind of clothing. My closet consists of black, gray, and khaki Dockers. Shirts are burgundy, black, and blue, short sleeve for when it's warm and long sleeve for when it's cold. They always look exactly the same. No one can tell whether I just went shopping or I'm wearing something I bought in 1990.

I'm thinking of trading them all in for outfits that consist of a sideways cap, a scarf, a white, sleeveless T–shirt, no socks, moccasins, and pants built for two. Come to think of it, I don't want to steal the thunder from the Beibs, so I don't know.

Hair

Every few months I go to my barber and tell him the same thing: use the number two guard all the way around. The entire "cut" takes about two minutes. Probably out of guilt, he tells me jokes and stories to put on a good show, making it seem longer so that his fee doesn't equal the hourly rate of a high-priced attorney.

I'm thinking of letting my hair grow until I can make a ponytail. The problem with that is my hair grows so slowly that by the time I get a ponytail, it will just piss off my CNA when he or she has to wash it, or when it gets tangled up in the back of my wheelchair. So, I don't know.

Tatoo

I'm not a fan of needles, especially when they're pointed at me, but this would be a lot quicker than the hair thing. I would have to place a tattoo where it can be easily seen by more than just all my doctors and sometimes my wife. My thought was to have a heart with my wife's nickname, Pixie, on my bicep. But my arms are so thin that with my luck only the first two letters would fit. Then everybody would think I'm a nerdy math fanatic.

I could just leave it alone. I do have a large mole on my back that resembles the full body profile of Alfred Hitchcock, or possibly Dr. Phil. However, I would have to take my shirt off for people to see it, which poses a whole new set of problems; not to mention I should probably have it looked at by a dermatologist. So I don't know.

Piercing

Like the tat, the piercing would have to be visible most of the time. I'd probably have to do something either on the side of my nose or right at the nostrils. But because of allergies, I blow my nose so much, I know I'd be constantly dabbing at the glistening thing, thinking something from inside my nose had escaped to the outside of it. So I don't know.

In case you're curious, the "celebrity" mentioned in this chapter's title is to make me feel good about myself just in case these other things don't work out.

A Word to the Wise

It's bad enough that I have to put my bladder's needs above my children's needs, but I'm also ashamed to say that I have not handed down any words of wisdom to my sons. And I have continued the legacy with my grandchildren. I haven't come up with any snappy axioms that they can live by and pass down to their kids.

My father didn't exactly give me any nuggets to work with either. All I can remember is that when he taught me to play cards, and I would lose control of the deck while shuffling, he would say, "Beware of sloppy dealers." I suppose that could work as a metaphor about life. Maybe the message is that there are people who are seemingly fumbling and stumbling innocently. They look like they are trying to give you a fair shake, but in reality they are trying to screw you.

My dad was a lot more literal than that though. The only other thing he ever said was, "Don't take any wooden nickels." That doesn't even work today because the lumber it takes to make a wooden nickel is worth way more than five cents.

Even my childhood hero, Fess Parker (aka Davy Crockett) was not helpful. He often repeated the quote, "Be always sure you are right—then go ahead." Really? That's it? I can say this with a great deal of certainty: there are a ton of people in this world who are absolutely convinced that they're right, but when they go ahead, the result is utter disaster.

So where does a guy turn for inspiration and guidance? When I'm looking for deep thoughts and pearls of wisdom, I look at, what else, oldies pop music lyrics. Somewhere in the songs that I've listened to for decades, there must be something that my descendants can live by. Here are some pieces of advice and philosophy that have helped shape the person I've become.

- Happiness is a warm gun.
- If the house is a-rockin', don't bother knockin'.
- It's hip to be square.
- Life ain't easy for a boy named Sue.
- Good girls don't.
- You're gonna need an ocean of calamine lotion.
- Everybody's working for the weekend.
- People are strange.
- Scotch and soda.
- You're riding high in April, shot down in May.
- Breaking up is hard to do.
- If you want to get to heaven, you have to raise a little hell.
- First there is a mountain, then there is no mountain, then there is.
- There must be fifty ways to leave your lover.
- Saturday night's all right for fighting.
- Mama's got a squeeze box; daddy never sleeps at night.
- Bottle of wine.
- Bang on the drum all day.
- Catholic girls start much too late.
- If you go carrying pictures of Chairman Mao, you ain't gonna make it with anyone anyhow.
- Oz never did give nothing to the Tin Man that he didn't already have.
- Just beat it.
- Everyone knows it's windy.
- Electrical banana is bound to be the very next phase.
- Tequila.

- You don't spit into the wind.
- There ain't no cure for the summertime blues.
- Don't waste your money on a new set of speakers. You get more mileage from a cheap pair of sneakers.
- Chug-a-lug, chug-a-lug.
- I know it's only rock and roll, but I like it.

I'm going to gradually reveal these pearls to my kids and grandkids. Someday, when I'm gone and I'm talked about, someone will say, remember when Dad/Grandpa used to say, "The bird is the word?"

"Yeah, I do. He sure was an idiot."

Idiots Unanimous

"Hi, my name is A. G. Sloan, and I'm an idiot."

"Hi, A. G."

My first recollection of my stupidity was at age five when the song "The Ballad of Davy Crockett" was popular. I could never figure out how Crockett went on to be a congressman and a hero of the Alamo when he was killed in a bar when he was three. What was he doing in a bar at that age, and who would want to kill a three-year-old? These were the burning questions plaguing me. Years later, I realized the lyric said "kilt him a b'ar (meaning bear) when he was only three."

OK, you might say, "You can't judge yourself on how you were when you were five." How about as a preteen? I was in the car with my dad, and I was asking him about passing other cars. He explained spacing and the timing of getting around a car and having a safe distance from an oncoming car. Another time in the car, I noticed yellow "No Passing Zone" signs. I kept trying to figure out how the people who put up the signs knew that a car would be coming from the other way. Thankfully I didn't declare this out loud. My father would have thrown me out on the side of the road like an unwanted pet.

Moving ahead to high school chemistry, our class had to do some kind of science project. We were to pair up with a partner. There were sixteen students in the class, but everybody seemed to have someone with whom to work except me.

Anyway, this put me on my own. I was then, and am now, science-impaired. I'm still trying to figure out that volcano thing. With absolutely no help, direction, or knowledge, I resorted to looking at an old science book I found in my parents' basement that was dated, I think, 1949. I can't be sure because the copyright was in Roman numerals.

I didn't understand anything in the book, so I picked the part that I thought required the least amount of work. I simply copied some formulas (or do I say formulae?) with mathematical and scientific symbols that looked like cuneiform, which it may have been considering the age of the book.

I threw together some posters with all this incomprehensible mumbo jumbo with no real purpose or conclusion. The night of the science fair, I tried to leave my station as often as possible as people passed by so I wouldn't have to answer any questions, which I couldn't have done anyway. My parents found me, though, and I had to, of course, show them my project. My parents didn't have much school education, but their faces indicated to me that they realized I had no idea what I was doing.

Then one of the judges wandered over to my space. She looked friendly enough. She smiled as she approached my table and asked, "What do you have here?"

As I began to speak, I swear I heard my voice come out sounding like the cartoon character Goofy. "Well, these are just some postulates and theorems, uh huh, uh huh, yep, yep."

"Could you elaborate?"

"Well, here on *this* poster are some postulates, and on this *other* poster there are some theorems." She was nice enough to let me off the hook.

Now in my adult years, I have no confidence at all in my ability to think. I defer to other people who seem more in tune with common knowledge, more specifically, my friend Terry. He knows everything, so I simply adopt his ideas. Here is a sampling of his beliefs that he seems to have a ton of proof for:

Aliens and their offspring live at Roswell. There is no global warming, but the government does use chemtrails to control the weather. Lee Harvey Oswald did not act alone; his accomplices were Russia, the Mafia, Cuba, the CIA, and Lyndon Johnson. Dinosaurs are not extinct; they still roam the jungles of Africa. The first moon landing was filmed at a Hollywood studio and directed by Stanley Kubrick. Paul McCartney "blew his mind out in a car" and would have been twenty-eight in 1970 if he had lived, because when you play "Revolution 9" from the White Album backward, it says "turn me on dead man." And there is a concentration camp under the Denver International Airport.

These ideas sound kind of weird, but what do I know?

The State of Matri-Money

The average cost of a wedding is now about $30,000. Let me put that in perspective for you. Thirty thousand dollars is a shitload of money. Maybe that's not helpful. Let's put it this way. One could buy a very nice, dependable car that, and, no offense, according to actuarial tables and other incomprehensible statistical analyses, has a very good chance of lasting longer than a marriage. Plus, you can sell the car and actually get something back for it. Try that with a wedding.

It doesn't have to be this way; that is, the costs don't have to be this exorbitant. No matter who is paying, with just a little tweaking, your wedding can still be the memorable event you want it to be but for a more reasonable price tag.

1. **Venue**. No need for some fancy-schmancy room with carpeting and chandeliers. Stake out some farmers' fields, find the most remote spot, and put up a big party tent.
2. **Music**. Forget a band. They will take advantage of the food and drink. Because they belong to a godless, corrupt union (my mother's words, not mine), they will play for forty minutes and take a break for twenty. This is when they will be eating and drinking. Forget a DJ, too. No need to pay someone from several hundred to thousands of dollars to play "Celebration" and emcee the bouquet toss. Ask someone to bring an iPod and iPod dock, put it on shuffle, and forget

about it. It doesn't matter whether you ask someone who has mostly songs by Daft Punk or Perry Como; the outcome will be the same. People will leave soon after the music starts. This helps with...

3. **Liquor**. The sooner people leave, the less the bar bill. The only other way to go cheaper is to make it a cash bar. The guests will drink less, but they will bad-mouth you for the rest of your natural life.

4. **Photographer/Videographer**. Everybody, even folks in their nineties, has a phone that takes pictures. At the end of the night, everyone simply sends what photos they took to the bride and groom. Also, instead of a videographer, hire a courtroom sketch artist. Many of them are out of work because of cameras in the courtroom, so they'll give you a good price. Make sure you don't get a police sketch artist, though, because then someone will have to be there to describe everybody to him. Very time consuming.

5. **Tuxedoes**. No. Men hate to dress up. They want to be casual and comfortable. If the bride insists on tuxes, the whole wedding party should wear black pants and those T–shirts that look like tuxes. Best of both worlds.

6. **Preacher**. Get someone in the family to go online to become a minister in something like The Church of the Infinite Sidewalk Crack. Hold the ceremony in the party tent. No church, no singers, no money.

7. **Invitations**. E-vites on Facebook. Anybody who is not on Facebook doesn't deserve to go to the wedding.

8. **Rehearsal dinner**. Rehearsal? We don't need no stinkin' rehearsal.

9. **Flowers**. Ask one of the invitees to specifically request "No flowers!" because, you'll say, they are allergic to every kind of flower that exists.

10. **Transportation**. Why? People have been going to weddings and going home after them since marriage began. How about a little individual responsibility?

11. **Wedding cake**. Everybody likes cake. Get a good one that everyone will like. Don't order anything weird like spumoni cannoli fudge nut cake. Get white and chocolate and make sure it's fresh. We do not want weird, dry cake. Understand?

12. **Food**. Don't skimp on the food either. That's all anybody talks about at a wedding except for cake. The money-saving aspect of food, however, is to have a buffet. Tell people they must go through the line with their place card and hand it in at the end of the food line. No returns to the line. Once through and done. You'll know exactly how much to order and will not waste anything.

13. **Favors**. Do us all a favor. Don't have any.

14. **Rings and bride's dress**. These two items pose the biggest threats to capping costs. Women like to show off their rings. It reflects badly on the groom if the ring is below standard. The rule of thumb is to spend two months of salary plus everything you have in the bank. Sorry, that is a hard-and-fast rule. Bride's dress? She's going to pick out what she *absolutely loves*. If she *absolutely loves it*, she just has to *have it*. It will be the most expensive one in the store, and she will get it. This is *her day*, which also means she might be the biggest stumbling block to attempting numbers 1-13.

The Long and Binding Road

My wife and I have jokingly pretended that our marriage is a series of one-year contracts. Inevitably, on or near our anniversary, one of us will ask the other if we will renew the agreement.

Just for the fun of it, this year we decided to actually haggle through the process of creating a contract to see what it would look like after forty-two years of marriage. Here is that document:

Part the First, the Preamble.

We the two people in this relationship, in order to form a more perfect UNION, insure DOMESTIC tranquility, provide for a way to DEFEND ourselves, promote each other's general WELFARE, and secure the blessings of LIBERTY (as far as that goes in a marriage), do ordain and establish this marital agreement.

Part the Second, the Articles.

Article 1. Both parties agree that once a week SEX is an admirable goal. However, both parties agree that there are times when it must take a BACKSEAT to other priorities, which may include, but are not limited to, reading a book, playing hearts on the computer, snacking, sleeping, watching *Blue Bloods*, *The Bachelor*, *The Good Wife*, or any major sporting event, which is defined in this contract as ANY sporting event.

Article 2. WIFE will not attach a toilet seat cover that compromises its ability to remain upright, thus putting HUSBAND in a PRECARIOUS position.

Article 3. WIFE will make every attempt to find qualified volunteers to accompany her on shopping excursions. If none are available, HUSBAND will accompany WIFE under these conditions: the entire excursion lasts no longer than two hours, not including drive time, HUSBAND does not have to answer more than a total of twelve questions, and HUSBAND does not have to stand. A chair must be available; otherwise HUSBAND is allowed to sit in the car or at the nearest DRINKING ESTABLISHMENT, if it is within walking distance, until shopping is complete. If HUSBAND must go to a DRINKING ESTABLISHMENT to sit, WIFE gets a total of four hours of shopping but also must drive home.

Article 4. If either HUSBAND or WIFE should CRITICIZE the other in any area, that job automatically becomes the new job of the CRITICIZER. If said HUSBAND says the mashed potatoes are too lumpy, it would then become said HUSBAND'S job to properly mash the potatoes.

Article 5. Meals will be cooked at HOME five days a week. HUSBAND will cook at least one of those meals but no more than two. If neither party feels like cooking, then GOING OUT or ORDERING IN will replace that thing about five home-cooked meals a week.

Article 6. HUSBAND will pay the BILLS, but WIFE will always have the checkbook, the debit card, the credit card(s), and all cash in HER POSSESSION at all times.

Article 7. It is understood that HUSBAND does not respond to MORNINGS as well as WIFE. It is also understood that WIFE has a great deal to SAY, mainly the things she has been up all night thinking about. Before WIFE goes to full-blown rattling off in great detail what's on her mind, HUSBAND should first be allowed to get out of bed and RELIEVE HIMSELF of liquid and/or solid waste.

Article 8. WIFE will use CPAP machine that currently resides somewhere in the corner of a walk-in closet. HUSBAND agrees to have a sleep study to find out why he SNORES too.

Article 9. When someone's family comes to visit, the person whose family it is by marriage may say that he or she has to RUN TO THE STORE to pick up a few things, but the absolute time limit is forty-five minutes, no matter where he or she really ends up going.

Article 10. Whoever drives the car CONTROLS the music system. The driver is not required to stay on a station playing "Hanky Panky" even if passenger says, "Oh, I like that song."

Article 11. Both parties will agree to SPEAK LOUDLY and distinctly to each other, and under no circumstances will either party still be speaking while WALKING AWAY from the other party.

Article 12. Both parties will IGNORE the noises the other makes, such as sighs, grunts, groans, slurps, sniffs, and chomps. Also, any faces that are made during the noisemaking, or any other time, are not to be taken personally because they are what they are and are NOT DIRECTED toward the other party.

Article 13. If WIFE wants to buy any ITEM for the house, she must DISCARD two other ITEMS.

Article 14. When HUSBAND has to FART, he will make every attempt to get as far away from WIFE as possible. It is agreed by both parties that WIFE has never FARTED.

Article 15. If WIFE precedes HUSBAND in death, HUSBAND would be FORBIDDEN to marry, date, be with, or look at another woman or else WIFE will HAUNT and TORMENT said HUSBAND. If HUSBAND dies first, WIFE will be able to marry but only for MONEY.

For the sake of full disclosure, I will tell you that we worked on these for THREE MONTHS and have not AGREED on anything except the PREAMBLE. Maybe NEXT YEAR.

A Day in the Strife

Ever since Adam and Eve were expelled from the Garden, were ashamed of their nakedness, and Eve turned to Adam and said, "Does this fig leaf make me look fat?" men have been subjected to shopping by women. I know it continues today because I too am a victim. And I know there are others, because I see them with the same look on their faces and the same body language and hear the same tone of voice as mine.

What we are mainly being subjected to during these excursions to the mall is akin to being in a police interrogation room all day. "Should I get this size blouse or the same blouse in a smaller size?"

"I don't know."

"Do you think this will fit so and so child?"

"I don't know."

"Do these jeans make my butt look thinner than the ones I showed you two hours ago?"

"I don't know."

I say I don't know to everything for two reasons. First, I really don't know the answer. I know less about clothes and sizes than I do the Higgs boson God particle. The other reason is if I say I don't know often enough, my wife will relieve me of shopping duty because I am no help.

That has not worked.

There is one question, however, that do I answer, and that's when my wife comes out of the fitting room holding a closet full of clothes and asks me how much money she can spend. At this point, I don't care if she maxes out every credit card we have and takes out a home equity loan as long as we are done.

But we are not. I get the "while we're here" phrase, indicating we have more stops. We enter a place that is so colorful that it looks like an explosion of fifty thousand kaleidoscopes. It's called Soaps R Us or something like that. And that's what it is, a place that sells nothing but kitchen and bath soap.

But it is not ordinary soap. They are specialty soaps called Bouquets of Fields of Heather Petals and Highlands of Hemp. My wife says, "Smell this. Do you like that?"

"I don't know." She knows I have weak olfactory glands. I can detect two smells, baby poop if I'm changing a diaper and skunk spray if I'm within eight inches of the skunk. If something is cooking on the stove, I couldn't tell you if it is spaghetti sauce or a Hannibal Lecter specialty.

"What about this one?" she asks as she holds up something called Apple, Peaches, and Pumpkin Pie.

"I don't know," but now I am getting hungry and have the urge to dance.

The other problem with the soap store is that one needs an advanced degree in math to figure out what the best deal is. (Get your calculators ready.) My wife has a coupon that says buy one get one for half price. The sections of soaps we are looking at are three for $14.89. But if we choose from a different table of soap, they are five for $24.95. A third section advertises twenty for $99.99. Twenty is even off the charts for my wife. We buy three, but we do not use the coupon because no one in the store can figure out how to apply it.

We make our way out of Soap City, through the mall, and into the department store, where my ordeal began just a short eight hours ago. But just before I reach the freedom of the parking lot, my wife stops to look at bras. She grabs a few and disappears into the fitting room, and I am stranded amid women's unmentionables.

There is no place that I am more uncomfortable and self-conscious, and this comes from someone who once played the accordion on a parade float. I cannot decide what to do. There is no chair. If I stand around near the fitting room, I look guilty of something, and if I walk the aisles, I look even guiltier. I feel the urge to tell the passing women that my wife is trying on bras, but it would sound like an alibi. I am in constant fear that a woman shopper will go to the nearest cashier and report that there is a pervert lurking in lingerie and maybe security should be called.

It is now 7:30 p.m., and we are eating dinner at a nearby Olive Garden. I am guzzling beer and eating one breadstick after another. My wife is reveling in the productivity of the day. I am seething as I keep repeating over and over in my head, "I am never doing this again. I am never doing this again."

I try to figure out if that's the sentence I want to say out loud when my wife says, "You're such a great husband to do this with me today. Do we have any time tomorrow to get a birthday present for your mother?" In a barely audible voice I say, "I don't know."

I Am Afraid of These Things

Prologue
The following should either be recited or sung keeping in mind the
song "We Didn't Start the Fire" by Billy Joel. Thank you, and now,
I Am Afraid of These Things.

Gonorrhea, West Nile, Judge Judy, tainted bile
Salmonella, listeria, attacked by a drone
Bubonic plague, the guillotine, dehydration, hammer of peen
Botulism, impetigo, rays from my cell phone
Whooping cough, anthrax, chicken pox, shark attacks
Ricin, the number nine, falling in a vat of wine
Norovirus, rock slide, poisoned by cyanide
Hepatitis, meningitis, a cave-in at the mine

I am afraid of these things.
The world's so scary,
Not a bowl of cherries.
I am afraid of these things.
If there's anything else,
Just keep it to yourself.

Diabetes, pneumonia, shingles, and Ebola
Walmart shoppers, anxiety, obesity
ISIS, tetanus, Tourette's syndrome, skin cyst

Encephalitis, mauled by a zombie
Car crash, herpes, getting cut off at the knees
Getting measles, common cold, burned at the stake,
household mold
MRSA, heart attack, an avalanche, the rack
Legionnaires, LaPierre, erectile dysfunction

I am afraid of these things.
The world's so scary,
Not a bowl of cherries.
I am afraid of these things.
If there's anything else,
Just keep it to yourself.

IRS, Parkinson's, hit by a bus, slapped by nuns
Bad burn, volcano, mangle foot when I mow
E-coli, going to hell, Mayor Emanuel
Choking on my own drool, drowning in a backyard pool
Buried alive, sinkhole, starvation, arsenic
NSA, hoosegows, knocked out in a bar row
Earthquake, killer bees, Kim Jong-Un, and Lyme disease
A house fire, mad cow, run over by a plow

I am afraid of these things.
The world's so scary,
Not a bowl of cherries.
I am afraid of these things.
If there's anything else,
Just keep it to yourself.

Alzheimer's, plane crash, bleed out from a large gash
Swine flu, bird flu, old-fashioned kind will do
Crazies of the far right wing, cancer of the anything

Stabbing, boat wreck, people who like Glenn Beck
TB, a groin kick, being a phobophobic
Mono kiss, making lists, any white supremacist

I am afraid of these things.
The world's so scary,
Not a bowl of cherries.
I am afraid of these things.
If there's anything else,
Just keep it to yourself.

Teen driver, cholera, outbreak of malaria
Scabies, tattoos, leprosy, Fox News
Smallpox, cheap lox, fall from bridge, Carnival cruise voyage
Very high cholesterol, overdose of alcohol
Struck by lightning, apnea, and mesothelioma
Arthritis, pertussis, SARS, stroke, syphilis
Diarrhea overload, schizophrenic episode
Illegal seizure and search, the Westboro Baptist Church

I am afraid of these things.
The world's so scary,
Not a bowl of cherries.
I am afraid of these things.
If there's anything else,
Please keep it to yourself.

The More Things Change

A recent poll shows that about 35 percent of people don't believe in evolution. Sometimes people are doubting Thomases and need to see to believe. So let's start with some small, concrete examples of the evolutionary process that everyone can understand.

Sleeping with your partner begins with both of you able to sleep well on a small couch, holding each other. Then you graduate to a double bed, onto a queen, and then a king. Eventually, for both of you to get any rest, one of you sleeps in the bed and the other on the couch.

Also in regard to sleeping, as a baby you sleep fourteen hours a day in two-hour intervals. As a toddler, you sleep ten hours uninterrupted. As a teenager, you sleep twelve hours uninterrupted. As an adult, you sleep seven hours uninterrupted. As an even older adult, you sleep fourteen hours a day in two-hour intervals.

As a kid, you eat whatever you want. As an adult, you start to look at the nutrition facts on foods you used to eat as a kid and can't believe you consumed so much crap. You stop eating this stuff until you realize food is not fun for you, so you say screw it and eat anything you want.

A woman's hair evolves through various lengths, starting with her natural color, to trying purple hair, to trying a blond wig, to trying her natural color with blond highlights, to natural color with red highlights, to having to dye her hair to her natural color, to finally settling on a nice shade of blue.

You play loud, subversive, dirty music that your parents hate, on a stereo console in the living room. They tell you to listen to something else or turn it way down. When you have children, you have an inkling that they are listening to subversive music with dirty lyrics. But you're not sure because you can't hear it because they are always walking around with earbuds on.

You begin as a great Olympic athlete and win the men's decathlon. You have a minor TV career. You aren't heard from for years until your family gets a reality show. The next logical step is to become a woman.

You have to sneak off into the night to find the dealer who sells you pot. Then, you can get it with a prescription. Finally, you walk into a store and off you go.

You watch TV in black and white on an 11-inch screen. Then you watch in color on a 25-inch screen. You watch on a 70-inch HD-TV with surround sound. Finally, you watch TV on the 6-inch screen on your phone.

You drink because it's forbidden. You drink because it relieves stress from your job. You drink because you have children. You drink when your kids leave home. You drink when you retire. Finally, you realize you don't need a reason to drink.

You are carted around in a stroller. You learn to walk. You learn to drive. They won't let you renew your driver's license. You stop walking. You are carted around in a wheelchair.

When you go out, you start late and stay out until dawn. Next, you go out at seven and are home by midnight. Finally, if you *do* go out, you start at four and are in bed by nine.

Snow White needed seven dwarfs, a huntsman, and a prince to save her from the evil queen. Cinderella needed a fairy godmother and a prince to rescue her from her evil stepmother and stepsisters. Anna and Elsa just needed sisterly love. And a man? Maybe, maybe not.

If this doesn't convince you, then I'll be a monkey's uncle.

How to Succeed in Sexual Harassment without Really Trying

Boss: (on the intercom) You may send in Miss Peters now.
(Employee Peters enters.)

Boss: Please, have a seat.

Peters: Thank you.

Boss: I, as you know, am Haywood Jablomi, the owner of the company. Even though I delegate the hiring to my supervisors, I still like to be hands-on with my employees. So after new hires have been here a while, I like to informally interview them to get to know who's working for me out there and for them to know who the man on top is. No pressure. Just informational things. If there is anything you feel uncomfortable talking about, just say so. I won't hold it against you. Is that fair?

Peters: Yes, sir. That's fine.

Jablomi: (looking through papers, to himself at first) OK, Sharon Peters. You have been hired in at an entry-level position. Everything going well with your supervisor so far? Is he helping you with your new position?

Peters: Oh, yes, he's been great. Very helpful and knowledgeable.

Jablomi: Good, good. That Hardman was good to find. He's really stood out from the rest. Are you from here originally?

Peters: No, Pennsylvania actually.

Jablomi: Whereabouts?

Peters: Oh, you wouldn't know it. It's a small town in Lancaster County. It's called Bird in the Hand. My parents run a bed-and-breakfast there.

Jablomi: Surprisingly enough, I *do* know where that is. I have family in that area. My brother Dick lives in Intercourse. Bird in the Hand is just a short jaunt to Intercourse. Do you have any hobbies? Pastimes?

Peters: Many. Maybe too many. I love golf.

Jablomi: Good. We've got some enthusiasts here. We can always use more. I played this morning. After eighteen holes, I can barely walk.

Peters: I'm also an antique collector. Kind of, anyway. I'm always buying and selling. It's more fun than a business.

Jablomi: That's something I don't know much about. You should drive by my house because I take my junk out by the street. I don't know if it's worth anything or not, but someone always comes to get it. What else?

Peters: I'm an avid swimmer. It's my main form of exercise. I used to be on my high school swim team.

Jablomi: (pulls a brown bag out of his desk drawer and pulls out something) Cumquat?

Peters: (shakes head in the negative while waving her hand)

Jablomi: I wasn't on a team, but I did eventually get pretty good at the breast stroke.

Peters: I also love to read classic literature, and though I haven't done much, I'd like to travel to exotic places.

Jablomi: Read any Balzac?

Peters: Yes, I love him.

Jablomi: If you get the chance, go to Bangkok. My wife and I went last year. Very intriguing.

Peters: I'll put it on my list.

Jablomi: I know that sometimes people in your department go out for a drink. Is that something you are amenable to?

Peters: Sure, I like a drink periodically. In moderation of course.

Jablomi: Again, no pressure. It has no bearing on the workplace, but we're pretty social. It's good to know you like a little cocktail now and then. Ever have a Woodpecker?

Peters: Can't say as I have.

Jablomi: It's a kind of hard cider. Pretty good actually. Well, I don't want to keep you much longer, but I do want to explain the basic philosophy of our company. Ever since Peter Gazinya, God rest his soul, and I started it all, we have always believed in the same principles. We want you to take chances, think outside the box. Don't ever think of any idea you have as too cockamamie to tell us. You'll find that we all work together. With that spirit of teamwork, we have found that there isn't anything around here that we can't lick. Any questions?

Peters: I hate to ask at this point, but I really need the day off next Tuesday. Ordinarily I wouldn't ask, but it's very important.

Jablomi: (looking at his calendar) Tuesday, next Tuesday. You need to get off on Tuesday. Boy, that's not looking like a good day. I've got a big project I need to whip out by five o'clock that day, and I might need as many hands on deck as possible. I'll get back to you as soon as I can. I'm going to have to think long and hard about it.

A Short Quiz or a Long Exam

A new study that I am pretending exists right now shows that there is a direct correlation between a person's view of the world and the number of friends one has. Sometimes we are not even aware of our attitude toward life and how it affects us socially. Here is a questionnaire that I am pretending is scientific and valid that will definitively tell you where you stand.

1. Your favorite Lincoln movie is
   a. Lincoln
   b. Lincoln the Vampire Slayer
   c. Killing Lincoln
   d. Lincoln Lawyer
2. When you flip on a light switch and the bulb goes out, you
   a. think it might have been prevented had you touched the switch differently
   b. think the bulb was bad and was going out anyway
   c. know something is definitely wrong with the wiring in your house
   d. believe someone has conspired to ruin your life.
3. If you voted in the Republican primary, and had the following choices, for whom would you vote?
   a. Ted Cruz
   b. Marco Rubio
   c. Scott Walker
   d. Rand Paul

4. Which of the following Beatles' songs is your favorite?
   a. "A Hard Day's Night"
   b. "All You Need Is Love"
   c. "Help!"
   d. "Here Comes the Sun"
   e. "I'm a Loser"
   f. The Beatles suck
5. In the classic psychology picture of a glass of water, you see…
   a. the glass as half full
   b. the glass as half empty
   c. What glass?
   d. That's not water; it's vodka

Points:

1. a. 2. b. 4. c. 1. d. 3.
2. a. 3. b. 4. c. 2. d. 1.
3. a. 1. b. 1. c. 1. d. 1.
4. a. 3. b. 6. c. 4. d. 5. e. 2. f. 1.
5. a. 3. b. 2. c. 1. d. 4.

Scoring:

5 points:
You act like you ate Eeyore after he ate Lewis Black. According to you, nothing will turn out right. You have no friends, although there are people similar to you. However, you'll never meet them because they are hunkered down at home watching Fox News and following the Cleveland Indians.

6–12 points:
You are a typical pessimist. You believe things are bad, but you soften your outlook because you drink hard liquor. You have two friends

that you sit around drinking with, bitching about work, politics, and optimistic people.

13–18 points:
You are a typical optimist. No matter how bad things get, you are thankful that they are not worse. You hang out with your three friends sipping wine, telling stories about how proud you are that your children are not in prison.

19 points:
You are twenty-four-hour sunshine. After a while, people need sunglasses to be around you, and eventually they just have to get away from your strong glow. You have many friends because you lend them money and don't care if they pay you back. They, however, can only take you in small doses, so from the large pool of friends, you see each of them only periodically. It wouldn't hurt you if, every now and then, you would say something that shows you are not totally in la-la land; such as, something recognizing how evil Isis is instead of telling people you admire how goal oriented they are.

Minority Opinion

There are a lot of things many of us don't understand: for example, the Chicago Cubs, why Hollywood continues to allow Adam Sandler to make movies, and a certain billionaire whose hair is just as inexplicable as his comments. But what really perplexes me is why everybody wants my, and everyone else's, opinion all the time. It seems we can't do anything without being asked how it was.

Some of you may be old enough to remember when a business, for example a restaurant, didn't have to ask how it was doing. If people showed up, it was assumed that people liked the food, the service was at least adequate, and there were no critter prints in the alfredo sauce.

Then they started with those comment cards. It was innocent at first. The card had three categories: Food, Service, and Cleanliness. Next to each one, the customer could check either Excellent, Good, or Shitty. There was room for specific comments below where, let's say my wife, might write that the server called me "Hon" every time she addressed me, put her hand on my shoulder once (too often), and showed too much cleavage while bending over serving me chicken noodle soup, so we (she) will never come back here to eat.

Now, as you pay the bill, they give you a website to log on to so you can answer a fifty-question exam that includes everything from ambience to the quality of the graffiti in the restrooms. Do we really have to give that much information about our "dining experience" at IHOP?

Does the airline I recently flew really want to hear from me about my last flight? Everything was fine until midflight, when we experienced cabin pressure loss where the masks come down. I turned to my wife, who always pays attention to the safety lecture, and she already has hers on while I was panicking, fumbling around with the mask and the tube, and she, shaking her head meaning "I told you so," finally decides to help me. While sitting there hoping the oxygen they promised is being delivered, I decide, considering the case of a water "landing," to start looking at the flotation device under my seat: learning how to put it on, wondering what I'm going to do if it fails to automatically inflate because I won't be able to manually blow air into it with the oxygen mask on. And to top it all off, throughout this entire ordeal the guy in front of me had his seat reclined.

It's everywhere. I go to the grocery store. With the receipt I get a slip of paper that gives me a website to once again rate my twenty minutes there. Plus the cashier's name is on the paper so I may reference him or her to make the same him or her feel great about having successfully rung up my twelve items while asking me how I am today.

On the telephone while on hold, the robotic voice asks me if I'm willing to take a survey about the upcoming call. I always wonder: if I indicate I'll take the survey, will they handle my problem differently? Will they be nicer to me? If I say I won't take the survey, do they then take the call and not give a shit because they know I won't be giving them any feedback? Just in case, I always indicate I will take the survey, and when it starts I hang up.

It's so ridiculous that soon the corner hooker, after a client has, um, finished, will hand him a card with a website to go to and rate his experience. Which of our ladies were you accompanied by? How would you rate your overall satisfaction with Cherry's performance? Which of the following services were a part of your experience? (Due to lack of space, I will not list the possible categories and the various degrees of satisfaction.)

As the saying goes, "Opinions are like neuroses; everyone's got one." But I'm not going to send you to a website to rate the content, grammar, and writing style of this article. Don't write me a letter or send me an email or a tweet or an Instagram. Don't like me on Facebook. If you have an opinion about this, at least this one time, keep it to yourself.

Cheap Thoughts by Hack Jandey

- Disney: the place where housekeeping can fold towels into the shape of Mickey Mouse's head and we say, "Wow, this place is great."
- I'm tired of seeing my last name on every fixture in every bathroom in this country and having nothing to show for it.
- A friend of mine was taking a walk the other day and was hit by a van from a physical therapy clinic. Accident?
- I'm such a loyal friend that to lose me as one you'd have to kill a member of my family, and even then it would depend on which one.
- I am a bundle of contradictions. For example, sometimes I'm really horny, but my hand is just not in the mood.
- Bad pickup line: I have some Viagra that expires tomorrow.
- How come some people emphasize that evolution is a theory, but they don't when it comes to the conspiracies they believe?
- Does anybody else find it ironic that Hooters sells wings and has flat-screen TVs?
- Beware of hospital ratings because they'd be a lot lower if the people who didn't make it out alive could fill out a survey.
- The inventor of Etch A Sketch died recently. Before they buried him, I hope they tried turning him upside down and shaking him.
- I have a smartphone, a smart tv, and a smart car, and people still call me a dumbass.

- I hope I don't get famous; I can't afford the drugs.
- Halloween is for kids. The rest of us have the entire year to pretend to be somebody we're not.
- I wonder if any apes are creationists.
- Whoever packs toys into boxes should be commissioned to secure our borders.
- As I get older, I find myself confusing things more often. I just called a friend and told him to meet me at The Tilted Hooter.
- You know those clips that keep an opened bag of chips fresh? Who keeps chips that long?
- They say the Roman Coliseum is starting to lean, a classic case of Pisa envy.
- You know the kid who saw his mommy kissing Santa Claus? It could have been a lot worse.
- I hit a car yesterday when I glanced up at the electronic sign that tabulates the number of traffic fatalities there have been for the year so far.
- A construction sign in Michigan: Kill or Injure a Worker, $7,500, 15 Years. I'd rather have it in a lump sum please.
- There used to be a laxative called Serutan. Their ad campaign used the slogan, "Serutan spelled backward is natures." That technique wouldn't work with every product, of course, like Subaru and Tums; but it sometimes could be effective. "Aren't you glad you use Dial? Don't you wish everyone did? And remember, Dial spelled backward is..."
- When people ask me if I'm a glass-half-full or glass-half-empty guy, I tell them I don't even see the glass.
- I'm one good lawsuit away from retirement.
- Went to an Immediate Care and had to wait for two hours. Should be called Eventual Care.
- We really have an epidemic (did you ever notice there aren't any cemeteries near hospitals?) of people with ADD.

- I'm writing a book called *Women Are from Bars, Men Are from Penis*.
- It'll be a hot day in Reykjavik before we all agree on climate change.
- There are three reasons why pot should be legalized: it has medicinal benefits, it...wait, what?
- All you crazies repeat after me: suicide-murder, suicide-murder, suicide-murder...
- I'm really glad the people who make shopping carts don't make cars.
- Aren't they really giving answers on *Jeopardy!*?
- The presidents that we know cheated on their wives were better at the job than those we don't think cheated.
- Has anybody checked with Native Americans about how they feel about Steak 'n Shake's Takhomasak?
- I've noticed that people get really angry if you compare them to Hitler.
- Climate-change deniers say the earth is just going through a cycle. I can't wait until it gets to rinse.
- I think that considering the way Christians behave sometimes that Jesus must be turning over in his grave.
- If Elvis was such a unique talent, how come so many people can imitate him? You never see any David Hasselhoff impersonators.
- The *Jeopardy!* Tournament of Champions is just another example of the rich getting richer. The tournament should actually be with those who were in the negative at the end of their match and didn't get to Final Jeopardy. It could be called The Tournament of Champ Peons.
- Why do so many Christmas songs have to end with a bar of "Jingle Bells"?
- On a whim I went to a Shoe Carnival...worst rides ever.
- I'm just smart enough to be able to explain to people how stupid I am.

- Why is it that fit runners keel over and die while Keith Richards goes on and on?
- All those crosses where there have been deaths from car accidents prove one thing: non-Christians are really good drivers.
- One late night after a few too many in a very dark bar, I ate a sandwich, and I'm pretty sure I ate the toothpick that held it together.
- Are joggers skinny because they run, or are people who like to run naturally skinny and would be skinny whether they ran or not?
- I've never watched *Duck Dynasty*. I'm trying to figure out what that says about me.
- Donald Trump is proof that to become a billionaire one doesn't have to be smart.
- I finally figured out what I want on my tombstone: "This Is *not* Funny."

Ninety Percent of Travel is Half Rental

I don't always just sit at home in my recliner and watch TV. Sometimes circumstances (my wife) force me to branch out and travel to other cities and stay in a hotel where I lie in a bed and watch TV. In order to do this, sometimes I have to rent a car.

The rental car process makes me uncomfortable. I feel a combination of guilt, stupidity, and determination. The people who have waited on me make me feel guilty that I am going to, I don't know, drive their car. I get the feeling they don't want me to because I am not trustworthy. I'm as trustworthy as the next guy as long as the next guy isn't Brian Williams. Also, the rental car company makes me feel stupid because they believe I need as much help as possible in deciding what's good for me, but I am always determined not to be taken.

My last experience, as usual, began online. After I made my airline reservations, I scrolled through the list of rental companies at the bottom. I, like any red-blooded cheapskate, clicked on the least expensive. The advertised price was $200 a week for a subcompact. When I arrive, I am met by a twelve-year-old who is dressed like a pit boss and has apparently just seen *Dazed and Confused* for the first time.

"We see that you have chosen our *no one really pays $200 a week* rate. All right, all right, all right."

"Yes, what kind of car do I get for that price?"

"It does not say car, sir. It says subcompact. That rate is for that go-cart over there. If you would like an enclosed vehicle that is allowed on the street, you will have to upgrade."

I am now up to $400 for a car that can fit a small duffel bag in the trunk and four people in the car, unfortunately all of them in the back. Doogie Howitzer continues.

"We have two kinds of insurance protection in case, God forbid, something should happen. Do you want the *basic* or *extreme*?"

"I don't want either one. I'll just use my own insurance if something happens."

"Well, sir, this protection is very cheap and protects you from, God forbid, all of the crazy drivers we have in..." (fill in whatever state you are in at the time. No matter where you are, they will tell you that their state has the worst drivers when in fact everyone knows that's Texas. Texans think that because their state is so large, they'll never run into each other on the road. They are wrong. Alaska would be like that too if there was more than just the Palin family living there.)

"With all due respect, you realize, sir, that your insurance sucks and will probably not pay out anything if, God forbid, something should happen. Are you sure you do not want to reconsider?"

"Yes, I'm accustomed to paying insurance companies that never want to pay a claim, but I don't need two of them."

"All right, all right, all right."

"Would you mind walking around the car with me looking for major dents?" I chose a black car, and we are in a dark, covered garage. I couldn't find my wife, who was standing two feet away, never mind any dents.

When I answer him, I say no. He looks at me funny, but that is the correct answer if I *am* going to help him look. These days, when you ask someone if they would mind doing something, they almost always say yes, or sure, or some other positive word. That means you *would* mind, which means you don't want to do what the person is asking. Wake up, people!

Anyway, we both pretend to be looking for dents and both conclude that we can't see any.

"How about a GPS? You do not want to get lost in a strange city where, God forbid, something might happen."

"No, thanks. The lady in the machine seems to deliberately lead me astray, so I have maps."

"I think I saw something like that when we cleaned out my grandpa's house after he died."

I say, "All right, all right, all right."

Then there is something about gas that I turn down. He begrudgingly says initial here, here, and here and sign here and here.

Lastly are his instructions about how to operate things on the car. He is so upset with me by now because I have not agreed to any of his upsells, except the bait-and-switch go-cart thing, that he tells and shows me everything on the car in fourteen seconds. All of a sudden, he doesn't care about my well-being and maybe not even the car.

"Here are the lights the air conditioning this is equipped with XMradio the seats adjust like this fix your mirror before you pull away windshield wiper sare here this pops the hood this pops the trunk the cruiseison the steering column along with bluetooth if you want to set that up so you can talkhands free this is the ejector button haha just kidding if you have any questions call1 800 your call is very important to us allrigh tall right all right."

Two minutes later, I'm on the road, and I can't get a reading on the gas gauge because it has no needle. Oh, well, what's the difference? I'm just going to stay in and watch TV anyway.

Play the Drunk Card

I'm sure a number of times in your life you've said things like, "Uncle Joe is a lot more fun when he drinks," or "My spouse does 'certain things' to me only when he or she is drunk." For the most part, we are better people when we drink. We laugh, we feel freer, we're more relaxed, we're more willing to let things go. Don't we want a world filled with people like that? We might drink a lot in this country, but I still don't think we use alcohol to its full potential. In an effort to make the world a better place, we need to put alcohol to better use in all facets of our lives.

My proposal is to reform our attitudes and laws about drunkenness and adopt a new form of identification called The Drunk Card. Here's how it works. The card has some of the usual pertinent information on it similar to a driver's license, but the main part of it involves four categories: (1) Spouse/Significant Other, (2) Family, (3) Friends, (4) Colleagues. Each of those categories has one of *four* designations: *drunk, sober, drunk with exception*, and *sober with exception*.

Your card is based on what other people think of how you act when sober and when drunk. So each of us will be at the mercy of others as to how our cards will read.

In categories *two, three*, and *four*, the magic number is five in each. If five people file affidavits that say you are a better person drunk in a category, you must always be drunk around all the people who comprise that group. If five people file affidavits that say you are a better person sober in a category, then you need to be alcohol-free around them at all times. As for category *one*, that person will decide—drunk or sober. If you are a polygamist, the majority will decide. If you have two wives, both of them would have to agree. If you have three wives, all will have to live with whatever the majority says, and so on.

If other people fill all four categories on your card with the *drunk* designation, it will be your new civic duty to be inebriated at all times: at home, at work, with friends, and with family, thus making the term "legally drunk" mean exactly what it says. If you have *sober* designations next to all four categories, you would never be able to drink again. Sorry, but this is about all of us being better people.

However, we know that life and people are not that simple. Not all of us are going to receive a card that has the same designation in each column. We, and the people who know us, are complicated creatures, so this legislation will account for that.

For example, one may get *drunk* in the first three categories and *sober* from colleagues. Perhaps they have seen you at office parties doing lewd dances and performing song parodies about the alleged viral warts on the boss's butt. If they think you are a better person sober, then so be it. You would have to be drunk everywhere except at work. Your card may have any combination of *drunk* and *sober.*

Even after you get all the necessary affidavits, individuals may apply for an exception. Let's say you have a *drunk* designation under family, but your daughter doesn't like it because, when you are, you constantly tell her that you think the guy she lives with is an even lower form of scumbum than her father. She can file an exemption indicating that when you are with her, you have to be sober. However, because you have the family drunk designation, when your daughter is outnumbered by other family members, you must be drunk, and your daughter will have to suck it up.

With any law, there must be consequences for breaking it. If you do *anything* to break other laws and you are not in your *drunk card* condition, no matter what the outcome of the other law you broke, you will go to jail for a year, no questions asked. As an example, you're with your brother-in-law Bob. You get into an argument with him when he says *The Brady Bunch* is still on the air. You say it went off the air in 1974. He tells you on what station you can watch the show. Therefore, it's still on the air. You push him; he pushes you back. A fight ensues. The police are called. You are supposed to be drunk around family, but you are not. Even if your brother-in-law drops the charges, you have to go to jail for a year. Had you been in your better, mellower state, you would have laughed it off, and none of this would have happened.

The *drunk card*—I know it's a good idea because I was really drunk when I thought it up.

The Sincerest Form Of...

My next project was going to be to write a novel. My mind is teeming with possibilities, but there is a danger. I have such an extensive literary background that maybe too much of what I've read will creep into my writing. The trick is to be creative while still paying tribute to other literary works, but since the "Blurred Lines" lawsuit, I'm a little tentative. Here's the CliffsNotes versions of a few ideas I've been pondering lately.

The Pride of the Yankees in King Arthur's Court
Lou Gehrig gets beaned at Yankee Stadium and is transported to the time of the Round Table. He teaches the men how to play baseball, and strikes out Merlin by throwing him, as everyone thought, magical curveballs. The people don't mind that the games take three hours, because, up to now, the main pastime for the men has been getting in and out of body armor.

And the women spend their days polishing it.

The Picture of Christian Grey
Christian Grey sells his soul to the devil in exchange for unlimited credit at Ace Hardware, but that has nothing to do with the main plot. One day, four of C. G.'s former "girlfriends," all still bearing scars from their relationship with him, kidnap him. They tie him to a bed, forcing him to watch Comedy Central and periodically dosing him with nitrous oxide. On the wall above the TV is a picture of Grey surrounded by some of his favorite things: a nail gun, nunchucks, and nail clippers. Every day the suit he's wearing in the picture changes to some hideous,

outdated one. One day it's checkered, the next it's a leisure suit, in patterns and colors only seen at a clown college graduation. The paraphernalia gradually rusts away, as does Grey's face in the picture and in real life. (Note: this is not so much a tribute as it is an attempt to cash in on something wildly popular, plus I think he's got it coming.)

The Invisible Man of La Mancha

Don Quixote, who can sing like the dickens, travels around with a guy named Griffin, who has found the secret of invisibility, all the while being pursued by the Don's mortal enemy, the Enchanter. Griffin inadvertently confuses Don's water with his potion, and Quixote drinks it and disappears. Invisibility affects Don's eyesight and apparently his brain because, of all the fun things one can do by being invisible, this guy chooses to attack windmills. Granted, they didn't know what hit them. Eventually, he is fatally wounded because, even though invisible, he sings "The Impossible Dream" so loudly that his enemy can figure out where he is and kills him.

I've got others in progress whose plots aren't totally developed. Here are some working titles:

To Kill a Mockingjay
Gone Girl with the Dragon Tattoo
Inherit the Wind in the Willows
Foxcatcher in the Rye.
Tiny Alice in Wonderland.
Treasure Island of Dr. Moreau.
The Jungle Notebook of Mormon
The Tell-Tale Heart of Darkness
Little Women in Love
The Divine Comedy of Errors
Steppenwolf of Wall Street

I hope I haven't shared too much. I guess I'll have to trust that none of you will steal my great ideas.

O Come Back All Ye Faithful

Pope Benedict XVI did something that a pope has not done for a very long time. No, he didn't get married; he quit. Shortly before he did, he stated that the Catholic Church needed to find ways to win back "lapsed" and "lukewarm" Catholics. With all due respect to the parting Pontiff, his observation is as obvious as the ass on Kim Kardashian.

But now the Church will have a new kid? on the block who will be faced with the same problem of trying to increase membership. He doesn't need to be reminded of the *one big problem* the church has had, so let's move on from that. There are other things he can do, and I am here to help him with them. I have a *ten-point plan* to bring fallen-away Catholics back to the fold and maybe even bring in some converts. It also gives me a chance to use Roman numerals.

I)   Don't call your people names like your predecessor. Lapsed? Lukewarm? Lapsed sounds like someone didn't pay his insurance premiums. Even though lukewarm contains the name of a gospel author, it still sounds insulting. While you're at it, eliminate the term "practicing Catholic." This identification gives members no sense of accomplishment. They never feel like full-fledged Catholics. Instead, use a ranking system that the average Joe understands, such as Apprentice Catholic, Journeyman Catholic, and Certified Catholic. For people who complete steps more quickly than whatever standard is set, there could be incentive bonuses such as papal blessings and long-term absolutions.

II)   Allow priests and nuns to marry, not necessarily each other. If the Church wants to have celibate clergy, the best way to ensure it is to let them get married.

III)   Choose popes by popular vote. The cardinals could be the Electoral College of Cardinals. If the people become discontent with the pope, they will at least have had a voice and be partially to blame.

IV)   Limit the pope's reign to ten years, or less if he can't last that long. People are more accustomed to watching their leaders voted out of office, overthrown, or assassinated rather than be in power for life. Ten-year terms allow the church to have living former popes, which we will have now. God knows how much revenue would flow into the coffers when ex-popes receive offers for autograph signings, speaking engagements, and a tell-all book. People would pay megabucks to hear the innermost secrets of any pope's administration.

V)   Forget infallibility of the pope. The pressure of always having to be perfect must be exhausting. Because the pope will be an elected official, he should be expected to be only as perfect as any other elected official. Well, maybe a little more perfect.

VI)   Modify the rule about going to church every Sunday. Watching Mass on television should count. Dad can simply DVR one "episode" of *Mass for Shut-ins* and watch it every week. This way he can watch at his leisure and not miss any of the important games that might be on. It doesn't hurt that he can eat a huge sandwich and drink a beer while he's watching.

VII) Revise communion. During the time of Christ, bread and wine must have been a natural combination. When's the last time anyone offered you bread and wine at his or her home? Why not other pairings? Beer and pretzels, coffee and cake, tea and crumpets, tortillas and tequila—the possibilities are endless. Each parish could build their own menus to satisfy their clientele.

VIII) Hire a public relations (not in the biblical sense) director. To prevent attendance from waning, a sports team usually has promotions to keep people coming back. The Church can do the same. It could institute giveaways like cross day, pennant day (a pennant with the name of a saint on it), replica pope hats, or special indulgences for the first two hundred people to arrive at a service. For more revenue, the giveaways could be sponsored, maybe a product that matches the item, like Double Cross Vodka and True Religion hats. Because of term limits, there could be an old-timer's day with all the living (obviously) former popes. What the church needs is to hire Mike Veeck, a baseball promotions genius, to consistently produce ideas that will have them standing in the aisles. Perhaps he would have an exploding altar that goes off during the consecration.

IX) Ok, just to be safe, altar boys and girls must be at least twenty-one.

There you have them, some very concrete suggestions to fix the Church. I've already sent these to the Vatican for the new pope. I know I said I had ten, but I lied. I hope he doesn't hold that against me, but I just think religious people are more attentive to a list of ten.

Increase and Multiply?

Why do people have children? No, seriously, why? I really don't get it.

Years ago, we were a rural country, so people had children to get more farmhands. The parents died at around the age of fifty, and the kids took over and had children of their own to keep things going.

But we don't work on farms anymore, except for the last bachelor, Prince Farming. We don't need children to create a workforce. So what is it?

I guess some people want to create little versions of themselves. Do they really want to have a mirror image of themselves staring at them every day? If they do, they're in for a rude awakening, because all they're going to get is a daily reminder of the things they hate about themselves. Do you want a little version of yourself? Commission someone to craft you a bobblehead doll.

Others may want to continue the family name. No offense, but names are more difficult to pass down these days. With the combination of divorce and trying to pay tribute to as many family members as possible, names are filled with hyphens and any number of middle and last names. The result is that sometimes no two people in the family have the same last name. A child's name today might be something like Albus Frodo Forrest Maximus Decimus Meridius Inigo Montoya-Dumbledore. You can't even lift that, never mind hand it down.

How about a tax break? The average cost of raising a child to the age of eighteen is estimated at $250,000. That's almost $14,000 a year, and you haven't even gotten to the college years, which, by the time a kid born today gets there, will cost about four million a year. All that pales in comparison to the measly deduction the government gives you for claiming a child as a dependent when you file your taxes.

I don't know if this is a reason people have children, but I've heard new parents say that they want to be friends with their kids. They start early, allowing their kids to banter with them. A typical exchange might go like this:

"If you loved me, you wouldn't make me eat this tuna casserole."

"But you know I love you."

"Yeah, but that's not what I'm going to tell people."

The parents somehow think this is cute and indicates that their kids are smart and sophisticated. Listen, your kids are three years old. They don't know shit, and if you think they do, then you don't know shit either. Your kids will have a lot of friends, probably way more than you. They don't need BFF's, they need BPF's.

There's always the possibility that people have a more profound reason, and they want to procreate to ensure that the human race will continue. Bwhahahahahahahahahahahahahaha. Sorry about that.

I don't know what other reasons there might be. I guess I'll have to do some more research. I'd start with asking my mother why she had me, but I'm afraid she'd say it was because of faulty birth control.

I've Got News for You

Other than the myriad of miscues that might occur, I make the same two mistakes every day: I read the newspaper and watch the news. Doing so on a daily basis has made me a nervous wreck. Everything scares me to death. Sure, there's that one nice story right before Letterman, Fallon, or Kimmel, about a dog that went missing during a family vacation three years ago and walked a thousand miles back to his home. The rest of it is scarier than having a three-way with Courtney Love and Steve Buscemi.

"Why don't you just stop?" you might ask. I can't. It would drive me crazier not knowing that there is discussion about a new fear. I need to know so I can adjust my behavior accordingly. I need these sources to tell me if there's listeria in my lettuce, salmonella in my sirloin, or a recall on my Rio.

It's a dangerous world out there, and the news won't let me forget it. They show me car wrecks and remind me that driving has never been safe. Flying is statistically the safest, but it never *feels* like it after watching the news. We are bombarded by the fact that Isis, or do you say Isil, is out to get us. They show me outbreaks of colds and flu. They tell me there are surfaces with norovirus on them and, currently, they're beating the *Ebola scare* drum. God forbid I get admitted to the hospital, because I'll pick up at least two additional diseases I didn't have before I went in.

I'd become an agoraphobic, but I'm told it's not safe to hunker down in my own home either. Somewhere behind my walls, my wiring might be plotting to ignite a fire. One of my gas pipes might leak, just for fun, and cause an explosion. Mold and radon gas might be conspiring in my crawl space to slowly do me in. My tap water has so many particles of whatever in it that instead of drinking it, I should chew it. Not to mention that the NRA reminds me that there is a home invasion every second in this country, and they are all happening in my neighborhood, so I need guns at the ready to stop these intruders in their tracks.

I feel trapped. There are mudslides, sinkholes, floods, tornadoes, and hurricanes more disasters than F-words in rap music. I can't go outside; I can't stay inside. I need the perfect place. But there is no perfect pla…Wait a minute. Of course there is. It's the happiest place on earth. It's…it's Disney World. Sure, there are some crabby kids there and even crabbier adults, but nobody cares about the news there. I've never heard anybody cough or sneeze there. I've never seen a gun or a reason for anyone to have one. I've never even seen a mosquito.

So Robert Iger, I plead my case to you. Give me a place to stay. It doesn't have to be in Cinderella's Castle, which is too close to the fireworks anyway. I'll take a shack on Tom Sawyer Island. If you want me to, I'll dress like Huck Finn's Pap and sit in a rocker on the front porch and wave to the tourists as they float by on the riverboat ride. Or give me a room at the Haunted Mansion. I could periodically pop out from somewhere and scare the bejesus out of young and old alike. I would even agree to stand in for one of the presidents at the Hall of Presidents. I am six feet tall and weigh about 195. With some makeup, I should be able to stand in for one of the forty-three. I'll sit or stand there all day. I don't care. I'll be a conversation piece. People will say, "They're supposed to be animatronic, but I swear I just saw George W. scratch his crotch."

Please help me. Disney is the only place I can get a good night's sleep. It's the only place where people from all over the world have fun together and aren't plotting something. And if and when I emerge from my accommodations, I'll be sure to wander only in Fantasyland.

Surely You Jest

I am pretty sure that most people believe that we live in an age of great uncertainty. They say that there is nothing on which we can count, not our leaders, our churches, our relationships, yada, yada, yada. They think the only certainties are death and taxes. Some would even doubt those. Fifty percent of Americans don't pay income tax, and we're all alive.

But my big question to these people is, "Are you sure?" I think there are things we can always, definitely, no changes, count on. So take heart, oh you of the unsure, for here is the definitive List of Certainties.

1) If you're home alone and in the bathroom taking a dump, someone will come to your front door.
2) If the cable or satellite guy tells you he'll be at your place between one and five, he will be there at five-thirty, and you will be taking a dump.
3) No matter how infrequently you click on *The Jerry Springer Show* as you are channel surfing, there will be two people standing up, pointing fingers, and yelling at each other. One of them will be naked.
4) Your friends have been in an investment for many years and making great returns. When you finally have enough capital to get in, the investment will tank.
5) You unravel your Christmas lights and check that they all work. They do, until you actually put them on the tree. One

faulty light will cause an entire bank to go out, forcing you to check them all.

6) All people at a wedding ceremony are secretly or otherwise opposed to the couple getting married.

7) Whenever there is any kind of political campaign, some white, male Republican (is there another kind?) will make an asinine remark about a women's issue.

8) The couch that you have in your house seems perfectly fine. When you decide to get rid of it and haul it to the curb, it looks like a piece of crap.

9) You get up three times in the middle of the night to pee. The next morning you have a doctor's appointment. The nurse asks you for a urine sample, and you can't even muster a trickle.

10) Adding "On Ice" to anything means it will suck.

11) When you DVR something and go out while it's on, no matter how hard you try to avoid it before you can watch it, you will hear the outcome.

12) Whenever there is a major astronomical occurrence, such as a meteor shower or an eclipse, you either do not live in the part of the world where it's visible, or it will be cloudy.

13) When you fly, no matter what airline, no matter your point of departure, no matter your destination, no matter what time of day or night, your gate will be the last one in the terminal.

14) The Cubs will never win another World Series.

As I said earlier, this is not a partial list. This is it, all of what you can be sure. Because of the definitiveness of the list, I suggest you cut out this article and enlarge it to poster size. Then place it in your front yard next to your Ten Commandments poster or your Proud Union Home sign, not that you couldn't have both. If you display the List of Certainties, you'll have cars slowing down in front of your house, and you'll be the talk of the neighborhood. I'm sure of it.

To Your Health

I recently was in the hospital for five days. Five days is the max because on the sixth day patients die: by their own hand. If they are on a higher floor, they take their I-V stands and throw them through a window and jump. Others manipulate the buttons on their adjustable beds until they configure to a shape that will squeeze them to death. If it's anything like my experience, they do this because they cannot face another day of the following:

5:11 a.m.:	A woman with a needle bursts into the room and says she has to take four vials of blood from me.
5:18 a.m.:	Another woman comes into my room and says she has to take six vials of my blood, and she has no idea who that previous woman was.
5:45 a.m.:	The nightshift LPN informs me that I have not urinated during her stay and that if I don't, I'll have to have a catheter.
5:45:30 a.m.:	I fill the plastic urinal to the top.
6:20 a.m.:	I order breakfast.
6:21 a.m.:	A doctor comes in to tell me that I shouldn't have anything else by mouth this morning because this afternoon I'm going to have a *very invasive test.*
6:27 a.m.:	Read.
6:28 a.m.:	Start to nod off.

6:29 a.m.:	The new shift nurses come in to introduce themselves. I have met them all before. They ask me if I need anything. I tell them the white board on the wall in front of me says bed rest. I tell them I need that. They laugh and walk out.
7:07 a.m.:	I receive six texts from friends and family saying they don't believe I'm sick, just hungover. I don't laugh at their diagnosis.
7:13 a.m.:	Another woman with a needle and a toolbox of vials says the doctor ordered eight more vials of blood before my *invasive test*.
7:19 a.m.:	I turn on the TV and discover early morning programming is as bad as the afternoon and evening.
7:32 a.m.:	My breakfast arrives. The cafeteria delivery lady starts to set it up as I tell her I can't have it. She looks at my food designation and tells me it's OK. I explain again that it's not. She uses the call button to get a nurse. The nurse comes in and tells her I'm not supposed to eat. The food worker apologizes and takes everything away.
9:01 a.m.:	The nurse comes in to hook my legs to these pads that squeeze my calves every thirty seconds. This is to prevent blood clots. I don't protest.
9:01:30 a.m.:	I jump every thirty seconds when my legs are squeezed.
9:07–11:00 a.m.:	They take my temperature, blood pressure, and ten vials of blood. I am beginning to see a pattern. I tell them I cannot continue to give blood because I'm getting weak. I suggest I'm running low. They laugh and walk out.
11:00 a.m.–1:00 p.m.:	I have fifteen visitors. I tell my story of why I'm in the hospital fifteen times. I become very tired and hungry. My story becomes more

	profanity-laced as I continue to tell it. My ten-year-old granddaughter is my last unfortunate visitor.
1:05 p.m.:	They come for me to give me the *invasive test*. I urinate first so I will not have a catheter. I will not be sedated.
1:10 p.m.–2:15 p.m.:	I am prepped for the test.
2:15 p.m.–3:09 p.m.:	I wait for the doctor.
3:10 p.m.–3:12 p.m.:	Doctor performs test.
3:13 p.m.–4:00 p.m.:	I wait for someone to take me back to my room. I am afraid to fall asleep for fear they will do another test without my knowledge.
4:03 p.m.:	I am back in my room.
4:04 p.m.:	Read.
4:05 p.m.:	Start to nod off.
4:06 p.m.:	The doctor comes in to tell me the afternoon test was inconclusive, and he's ordering *an even more invasive test* for this evening. I am to have nothing by mouth.
4:10–5:30 p.m.:	I read, watch TV, and do crossword puzzles while the I-T guy runs in and out trying to fix the intercom system. He cannot.
5:37 p.m.:	They come to tell me I am being moved to a new room where the intercom works. Flowers, cards, books, newspapers, iPod, cell phone, clothes, and shoes must be moved. I don't carry anything to my new room.
5:45 p.m.:	As soon as I get to my new room, food arrives. I tell the lady I cannot eat it. She says there's no restriction according to her records. I tell her about the doctor and my test. She calls a nurse. The nurse says the food is for the person who was abruptly "transferred" from my new room. The cafeteria worker takes away the tray of food.

6:00 p.m.:	Three large men come to take me to my *more invasive test*. I am afraid they will be used to hold me down during my procedure. They assure me I will be sedated. I look forward to it.
8:00 p.m.:	Back in the room. I am very groggy from the sedation. On my tray there is orange juice and crackers.
8:17–9:30 p.m.:	They take my temp, blood pressure, pulse, and, guess what? Twelve vials of blood. They tell me I hadn't eaten very much today. They ask if I need anything. I tell them I need to sleep, and these things squeezing my calves will not help that. They laugh and walk out.
10:00 p.m.:	I get my plastic urinal and put some water and orange juice in it.
10:20 p.m.:	The LPN comes in, takes the plastic container, writes down the amount, and dumps it in the toilet. She asks me if I need anything. I say no.
Sometime in the middle of the night:	I am relatively sure that some woman came in asking me if I wanted to donate blood for the blood bank. I don't know what I said, but I feel weak.
8:00 a.m.–3:00 p.m.:	I have to wait for everyone who has seen me during my stay to sign off that I am allowed to go home: doctors, nurses, cafeteria workers, the cleaning lady, visitors to my room, and any visitors to other rooms on my floor. The I-T guy is the last to approve.

I have been home for two days now, and I feel great. That's what happens. The hospital makes you so tired, sore, and broken down that, even if they didn't find out what's wrong, you automatically feel better, thus making you think that what they did must have helped. Excuse me if I'm skeptical.

16 & 61 for Men

I don't generally write for a specific demographic because I believe the wisdom I impart is universal. It transcends age, race, and gender. (I'm trying to keep a straight face.) But just this once I'd like to address men between the ages of sixteen and sixty-one.

I have an important message for you. Although there are forty-five years between the two ages, surprisingly, there really is no discernible difference between them. Your future is better than you think. Do not fear it. Don't worry. You're going to be fine. Here's why.

16—Your parents tell you that getting a motorcycle is out of the question.

61—Your wife tells you that getting a motorcycle is out of the question.

16—You tell your parents, siblings, teachers, and friends what to do because you have all the answers.

61—You tell your kids, grandkids, siblings, coworkers, and friends what to do because you have all the answers.

16—You don't exercise or eat right because you think you are invincible.

61—You don't exercise or eat right because you know you are not invincible.

16—You are thinking of your future in regard to what your career will be and ideas about someday starting a family.

61—You and your wife are thinking about retiring from your careers and moving to another state away from your family.

16—You're starting to shave.

61—You're starting to shave your ears.

16—On the first day of your high school football tryouts, you are tackled so hard that you hurt your back. Your doctor recommends that you not play football.

61—You join a sixty-and-over softball league, and you hurt your back while taking practice swings in the on-deck circle. Your doctor recommends that you not play softball.

16—You can stay up all night talking to friends, playing games, and chatting on the computer.

61—You can stay up all night pacing because you have a sleep disorder, which is fine because you'd be waking up to go to the bathroom anyway.

16—If you are naked and get interrupted by someone, modesty dictates that you would hurriedly throw on pants.

61—If you are naked and get interrupted by someone, modesty dictates that you would hurriedly throw on a shirt.

16—If a young woman drives by and sees your face, she might turn around to see you from behind.

61—If a young woman drives by and sees you from behind, she might turn around to look at your face, but she'll be really embarrassed that she did.

16—You are eagerly studying the rules of the road so you can pass your driver's license exam.

61—You are sitting in a room on a Saturday morning for traffic school, studying the rules of the road so you can get your license back.

16—When you see an attractive woman, you are aroused and get an immediate erection.

61—When you see an attractive woman, you are just as aroused, but you have the erection about three days later.

16—You like to listen to your music at a high volume.

61—You have to listen to your music at a high volume.

16—You spend too much time watching television.

61—You spend too much time watching reruns of the same shows you watched when you were sixteen.

16—You are angry because everything in the culture is geared to people older than you.

61—You are angry because everything in the culture is geared to people younger than you.

16—You do not have a good grasp on how to handle money.

61—You do not have a good grasp on how to handle money.

I repeat. You're going to be fine.

They're Playing Our Son

I recently bought a new car with a new kind of radio, at least for me. When playing the radio, the title and artist of a song continually scroll on the display. I told you it was new for only me. Usually it will work like this: The Christmas S, and then it scrolls to ong, and then to Mel Torme.

But most of the time, my radio will simply show The Christmas S. It does not finish a title or artist name if it doesn't fit on one screen. I do a lot of channel surfing, so I end up seeing some very interesting names of songs and performers.

"Great Balls of Fir..." by Jerry Lee Lewis.
"Do It or Die" by The Atlanta Rhythm Sect...
"Can't Take my Eyes Off..." by Frankie Valli.
"Pick up the Pieces" by Average White B...
"Welcome to the Jung..." by Guns and Roses.
"You Ain't Seen Nothing Yet" by Bachman-Turner Over...
"Under the Boar..." by The Drifters.
"Cruel Summer" by Bananaram...
"Treat Her Like a Lad..." by Cornelius Brothers & Sister...
"Sweet Baby Jam..." by James Taylor.
"Somebody That I Used..." by Gotye.
"Piece of My Heart" by Big Brother and the Ho...
"If I Were a Carp..." by Tim Hard...
"Papa's Got a Bra..." by James Brown.
"The Boy I'm Gonna Mar..." by Darlene Love.

"Spinning Wheel" by Blood, Sweat, & Tea...
"To the Ends of the Ear..." by Nat King Cole.
"On the Dark Side" by John Cafferty & the Beaver...
"This Magic Mom..." by Jay & the Americans.
"Land of 1000 Dances" by Cannibal and the Head...
"If I Had a Ham..." and "Puff the Magic Drag..." by Peter, Paul & Mary.
"Two Faces Have I" by Lou Christ...
"Something Happened on the Way to Heave..." by Phil Collins.
"After the Love Has Gone" by Earth, Wind, & Fir...
"Do the Funky Chick..." by Rufus Thomas.
"Come to my Window" by Melissa Ether...
"You've Lost that Lovin' Feel..." by The Righteous Broth...
"Slide" by Goo Goo Do...
"Hold My Hand" by Hootie & the Blow...
"In-a-Gadda-Da-Vida" by Iron Butt...
"Could It Be Magi..." by Barry Manilow.
"You're All I Need to Get..." by Marvin Gaye and Tammi Terrell.
"What's New Pussy..." by Tom Jones.
"House of Pain" by Faster Pussy...

I guess I can't listen to the radio in the car with kids who can read.

Water, Water Everywhere

I hate waterparks. I realize that literally more than hundreds of families visit these so-called places of amusement every year, but I would rather have a cystoscopy performed with a fireplace poker.

My aversion to these H2O horrors stems from an incident when my wife and I took our young sons on vacation to Wisconsin Dells, a town completely enclosed by four large walls and a roof, putting every attraction indoors. They felt they could make more money year-round rather than just in the summer, which in Wisconsin occurs sometime in July and lasts for thirty-eight minutes.

Back to the incident. We went to the largest such park at the time. My wife and I let the kids roam on their own, mainly because, when it comes to water, neither of us like to interact with it much. I cannot swim at all. My wife has some water proficiency, and she could save herself in a body of water as long as land is no farther away than three yards.

So the children went to find the ultimate waterslides, wherein they put you into a life raft and hurl you down a cornucopia-shaped tube, and you spin and swirl as if being flushed down a toilet. We, on the other hand, sought out the mildest slide we could find. Actually, it turned out to be the second mildest because we were too embarrassed to go on the easiest one. That one was a red slide about the height of Danny DeVito and whose apparent age range for use began at embryo. We moved on to one where at least the participants were ambulatory.

It was called Thunder Rapids. The name of it sounded more ominous than it looked from the ground. You begin by choosing an inner tube at the bottom and then walking up an endless flight of stairs to the top. There you get situated on the tube, and an attendant gives you a little push down a winding ramp until you reach a small plateau and splash into a small pool of water. There another attendant makes sure traffic keeps moving. Then you continue down another, similar ramp to another pool, and another attendant, puts you on the third leg of the journey, the steepest and fastest, that empties into a much larger pool.

My wife went first and glided swiftly out of my sight as I settled into my tube. The attendant gave me a little push, but soon into my first descent, the tube spun around. I was now leaning backward looking up at the top of the slide and the sky beyond. Before I knew it, I hit the first pool and toppled out of my tube. The attendant, who wasn't trying too hard to suppress a smile, asked me if I was OK. "Yeah, yeah," I mumbled. I collected myself, got back on the tube, and went to phase two, a repeat of the backward spinning, the crash and dismount, and the smirky smile.

I began my final descent in the same manner, backward. I went flying down, trying to keep from toppling over and finishing the ride without a tube. Rapidly I approached the end. The tube once again crashed into the pool. The tube bounced out from under me, and I went headlong into the pool and under the water.

As I lay there, my first thought was they had an attendant everywhere else; surely there would be one at the bottom who would see me thrashing about and come to my aid. But no. Then I thought, so this is how it ends, drowning in a pool of water at the bottom of a beginner's slide in Wisconsin Dells. My life started to pass before my eyes. I got as far as seeing my college transcript with the words "Academic Probation" stamped on it, when I felt my body trying to tell me something. The message must have come from my lungs as they were swiftly filling with water. My brain finally received the message: *this pool is only three feet deep. Stand up, you idiot.*

I struggled to my feet, emerging from the pool coughing up water and other indeterminate fluids from deep down inside me. I felt people staring at me as I reached for my tube and stepped out of the three-foot depths.

I found my wife, who was totally unaware of any problem, somewhere beyond the sea of people standing behind the pool. She was smiling. "That was fun, wasn't it? You want to go again?"

"No, no. If you want to, go ahead. I'll wait down here."

Standing at the bottom of the slide just behind the endpoint of the ride, I observed person after person coming down the last ramp, facing forward, smiling, hitting the water, and then slightly jumping up out of their tubes and landing on their feet. I hate waterparks because they hate me.

Your Body Is a Wonderland

Dear Graduates of all High Schools and Colleges, None of Which Would Ever Invite Me to Speak for any Occasion:

Do you want to be head and shoulders above everybody else? Do you want to get a leg up on the competition? Do you have your heart set on being successful? Then lend me your ear.

First of all, you have to put your nose to the grindstone. You can't drag your feet. You must bone up on important information. Knuckle down and use a great deal of elbow grease, and in the twinkling of an eye, it's a no-brainer that this will give you a head start in putting your best foot forward.

You have to have the stomach for the interview process. Even though your knees might feel like Jell-O, you must keep a stiff upper lip. Get off on the right foot by rehearsing the interview ahead of time. This will prevent you from being tongue-tied. This is your only chance to get your foot in the door, so you don't want to put your foot in your mouth. If the interviewer has uncovered any of the skeletons in your closet, don't bury your head in the sand. Don't tiptoe around on your answers. Keep your chin up and don't be afraid to stick your neck out. Get everything off your chest. Make a clean breast of it, and don't try to pull the wool over anybody's eyes.

Once you get the job, the rule of thumb is to shake a leg and keep your hands clean. You want to get the thumbs-up from the boss, so you'll have to break your neck to prove yourself. You might have your back against the wall as the new blood.

You also have to avoid getting in the hair of your colleagues. Make sure you don't have a chip on your shoulder. There are those who will automatically go for the jugular. No matter, you have to rub elbows with them, but watch out for those who might want to stab you in the back.

There will be people who are a pain in the neck. They'll talk behind your back and maybe even give you the cold shoulder. Most of the time, you have to bite your tongue and not waste your breath. You're not always going to see eye to eye with everyone, but sometimes you have to let what they say go in one ear and out the other. Make no bones about it; soon you will feel it in your bones that you have taken the upper hand.

In conclusion, you want to get to the point where you're not looking over your shoulder all the time. Don't look down your nose at others. Toe the line and demonstrate that your head is screwed on straight. Eventually you will be an old hand at your job and hit the nail on the head in your profession.

I'm not pulling your leg when I say I have racked my brain to give you this heads-up. My intention was not to ram it down your throat, but I really hope it didn't fall on deaf ears.

Presidential Name Game

Recently, my fifth grandchild was born, and it got me thinking about the 2016 presidential campaign. First of all, I don't think it's fair that right after the midterm elections, we have to go cold turkey on political ads. I think they should get right to it so there is no down time. Each party should just run negative ads about people they believe will throw their hats into the presidential ring. Keep the momentum going, and give the American people what they apparently crave.

But I digress. My latest grandchild is a boy, and his name is Warren. His parents said they wanted a name that sounded strong, a male name that suggests a person in the boardroom (think Warren Buffett), or in the White House (Warren G. Harding). Even Warren Oates as Sergeant Hulka in the movie *Stripes*, when he tells Psycho to "Lighten up, Francis," fills the bill.

Getting back to the election. Using a little history and the idea that a name may be able to determine future success, I believe I can predict who will be the next president of the United States.

Jeb Bush. His name sounds like that of a southern Civil War general, which only plays well in certain parts of the country. We need someone more universal. In addition, his last name is Bush. We've already had two Bushes (ha-ha, giggle giggle) in the White House. We've had other pairs: two Roosevelts, two Harrisons, two Adamseseses, two Johnsons (knock it off; you're so immature), and two Clevelands. OK, he was the same guy, but he counts twice. But two seems to be the cap. Jeb is out.

Marco Rubio. Someone will inevitably pull a Jimmy Carter when he introduced Hubert Humphrey as Hubert Horatio Hornblower. Someone in the party will introduce him as Marco Antonio Polo. After that, people will then always think of that stupid swimming pool game instead of the man. Marco (Polo) is out.

Rand Paul. Everybody knows it should be Paul Rand. President Paul sounds too informal for a president. It works only for a pope. His father tried, and it didn't work for him. Rand is out.

Chris Christie. Although he could use the Taft tub, he's in the same boat as Paul. Plus, he has the added handicap of his first name being continued into his last name. We've never had that. No Donald Donaldsons, or Harry Harrisons. Chris is out.

Joe Biden. Joe's the kind of guy who walks into a room and, as he shakes hands, says, "Joe Biden, damn glad to meet you." His name is already familiar to us. We've already been calling him Vice President. All we'd have to do is take off vice, and it would still sound perfectly normal. What he doesn't have going for him is that we haven't had a former veep become president since George H. W. Bush. There was that thing with Al Gore, but, you know. Joe is out.

Mike Huckabee. President Huckabee? Really? Mike is out.

Rick Perry. His name makes absolutely no difference. Rick is out.

Ted Cruz. Ditto.

Trey Gowdy. I don't know if this guy's going to run, but I have a friend who, at the end of all of his e-mails, adds Trey Gowdy 2016. I assume he means for president, so I'll address his candidacy. Sorry, but Trey is a wimpy name. The only other previous presidential first name that is similar is Millard. That may have played in the middle of the nineteenth century but not today. Trey is out.

Scott Walker. I see a possibility here if he chooses a running mate who is married, gay, a union member, and will answer questions about evolution. Otherwise, nah.

Elizabeth Warren. The American people love to be a part of history. We'd love to have another first. She has a first name that conjures up power and royalty. And how about that last name! She is a formidable candidate although she maintains she will not run.

Hillary Clinton. She has the woman requirement, but she has an extra boost. People like me will vote for her just to have Bill be the first first man. He'll be out there smiling, pressing the flesh, so to speak, and reminding people he used to be president while telling us that Hillary won't let him in the Oval Office.

I'm sure there are others who I have failed to mention, and there will be those who will crawl out of the woodwork (maybe literally) to run. However, using my vast knowledge, the winner of the 2016 presidential election will be somebody named Hillary Warren or Elizabeth Clinton.

However, in 2052, watch out for my grandson Warren.

Bombin' Core

We hear a lot these days about the new common core standards. To put it mildly, people don't seem to be very happy with them. They think they are convoluting the simple, thus leading our children to more frustration than enlightenment.

However, I think many critics are basing their harsh judgment on little or no concrete evidence. Using my inside education connections (I know a custodian), I have procured a few questions from the actual tests spanning various grade levels. I report; you decide. (Sorry, I couldn't think of another way to put it.)

1. What is the difference between Keynesian economics and supply-side economics?
   a) The names.
   b) About $4.25.
   c) Nothing, in that neither of them seem to work.
   d) What?
2. The age of the earth is
   a) 6,000 years.
   b) about the same as Larry King.
   c) 4.5 billion years next Thursday.
   d) I'm confused because my dad told me one thing, and my teacher told me another.
   e) I don't need to know it because nobody cares about science.

3. If Rich Guy 1 can bribe Congressman A in seven minutes using one million dollars, and Rich Guy 2 can bribe Congressman B in five minutes using $700,000, who is better at taking a bribe?
   a) Congressman A.
   b) Congressman B.
   c) Neither, because they should have held out for more.
   d) Both, because one of them will eventually be told by a staff member in charge of bribes that one of the rich guys has to give him more money.

4. Describe the symbolism in T. S. Eliot's "The Love Song of J. Alfred Prufrock."
   a) Prufrock's indecisiveness could represent a kind of hell or purgatory.
   b) Ha-ha, you said Prufrock.
   c) Poetry? Poetry is dead.
   d) Really? What do you think your rap music is?
   e) Rap music? Poetry? I don't get it.
   f) Of course you don't.

5. What does the euphemism "enhanced interrogation" mean?
   a) Your mother is talking to you after you came home late.
   b) You're on *60 Minutes.*
   c) You're applying for a mortgage.
   d) The previous administration is "being economical with the truth."

6. What was William Howard Taft's middle name?
   a) Is this a trick question?
   b) We never studied this.
   c) We don't have to know this because nobody cares about history.
   d) Prufrock.

7. A pie chart
   a) is shaped like a sheet cake.

b) shows the number 3.14.

c) starts with a big letter E.

d) resembles Chris Christie.

8. Who is credited with having said, "Give me liberty or give me death?"

a) Neil Patrick Harris.

b) Dan Patrick

c) St. Patrick

d) Henry Winkler

e) Isn't this another history question?

f) Nobody in their right mind would say something like that.

9. What's the difference between a sine and a cosine?

a) Your credit score.

b) One gets directly to the point while the other goes off on a tangent.

c) A sine is the ratio of the length of the opposite side to the length of the hypotenuse. A cosine, not so much.

d) co.

10. *The Comedy of Errors* is

a) Congress.

b) written in something other than English.

c) a Shakespearean play based on the Chicago Cubs.

d) Congress.

e) Come on. You've got to at least get this one right.

11. Which of the following sentences is correct? (1) I could care less about the Koch brothers. (2) I couldn't care less about the Koch brothers.

a) Could care less.

b) Couldn't care less.

c) Either way, as long as you understand that I don't care about the Koch brothers.

d) By the way, how do they pronounce their name?

12. What mythological character was responsible for releasing all of the evils into the world?
    a) Posthumous
    b) Diabetes
    c) Limbaugh
    d) Sirius, Sonos, Pandora, or someone having to do with music.

13. Why are planets shaped like balls?
    a) Seriously, another science question? Don't you realize there are people (you know who you are) who could care less or couldn't care less about science?
    b) Because they were discovered by men.
    c) They're spheres, not balls, you dork.
    d) One of the planets is not shaped like a ball.
    e) Do I have to say it?
    f) No, we've given everyone enough of an opening to figure out the whole answer.

14. Which of these would not be considered an oxymoron?
    a) Reality TV.
    b) Business ethics.
    c) Sit on a potato pan, Otis.
    d) The guy on the OxiClean commercial.

15. Some neighborhood teens have a garage band called the Snot Bubbles. They are arguing about the wording for the title of their first album. Which of the following titles would be correct?
    a) *Here Come the Snot Bubbles*
    b) *Here Comes the Snot Bubbles*
    c) *Don't You Think You Should Record a Song First?*
    d) *I Can't Wait for the Snot Bubbles to Move Out of My Neighborhood.*

Stay tuned; my connection is working on getting the answer key.

What to Expect the Sixty-Fifth Year, Chapter 4-"The Male Retiree"

Fate has paired you with a recently retired sixty-five-year-old male retiree. We thank you in advance for your service. This chapter deals with the care and handling of this new male senior that will help you cope no matter what your specific relationship to him might be.

Feeding

We cannot emphasize this enough; you will need a *lot* of food. The typical feeding schedule for your senior is as follows: breakfast, late-morning snack, lunch, late-afternoon snack, dinner, late-evening snack, and middle-of-the-night snack. If your senior is not eating seven times a day, consult a physician immediately.

Sleeping

Your retired senior should also follow a specific pattern of sleeping. Sleep will usually occur while your senior is watching TV or reading. Sleep will also come upon him right after eating. Essentially, the only time that he will not be asleep is during the night, except right after his middle-of-the-night snack.

Growth

It is not unusual for your senior to begin to shrink. There is no hard-and-fast rule about how much height loss may occur. The best thing to do is not ever measure the senior's height. If he says he is six feet tall, let him continue to believe it, even though you'll know he is barely five-eleven. At the same time his stature is diminishing, your senior's weight will be increasing exponentially. This is called the "Where to Wear the Belt" phase. He will have to decide to hike up his pants above the middle bulge or lower them to well below it. This is a very important personal decision. It is best that you not interfere with it or comment on it after he has made his choice.

Hobbies

Sometimes a newly retired senior male goes a bit overboard with the idea that he is retired, and therefore he will not be doing *any work*. He might very quickly start to hire out his jobs such as lawn care and snow removal. There is nothing inherently wrong with this as long as it does not pose a financial hardship. However, he will soon discover that when he is not eating or sleeping, he doesn't have that much to do. This is when he might take up a hobby. There is nothing wrong with this in and of itself either. A good hobby will keep your senior active and involved. However, it is important that you attempt to guide him in the right direction. Keep him away from hobbies that cost money and time, possibly yours. For example, he may take up collecting vintage bricks. This may take him across the country to attend brick conventions, talking to other brick collectors, and eventually filling the garage, and possibly a room in the house, with bricks. Instead, get him into something that takes little money and very little room, something like humor writing.

110

Immunizations

He will need his shots. There are many that are recommended for seniors: flu, pneumonia, shingles, tetanus, whooping cough, meningococcal, hepatitis A–Z, and so on. He will not want any of these shots except maybe shingles because Terry Bradshaw told him that shingles are very painful. You will have to bribe him and then fool him. Tell him you're taking him to the zoo or a strip club, and then say you must stop at the pharmacy for a disposable camera (because that's what he uses). Get him in by telling him he can pick out some candy, and then get him to sit in a chair by the pharmacy where he will get his thirty-two shots.

Doctors

He will need to see many doctors: primary care, urologist, cardiologist, dermatologist, hematologist, ophthalmologist, and dentist to name just a few. He will not want to go. See *immunizations* for the recommended method of getting him there.

Exercise

You can buy him exercise equipment for the home and/or give him a gym membership. He will not use either. The best you can hope for is that retrieving the newspaper in the driveway and his numerous trips to the kitchen will suffice as exercise.

Senior-proofing

This does not mean that you must put rubber pads on the corners of the coffee table or cover the electrical outlets. However, he will be wandering at night, and out of deference to others in the house, he will be doing this in the dark. Make sure his path from the bedroom to the kitchen is clear. Don't leave the vacuum cleaner in the hallway or shoes on the stairway.

Potty
He will be spending short and long periods of time in the bathroom because he has to urinate, defecate, or wants to read or just sit. If he has just finished eating, he may also be asleep in there.

Television
For some reason, and unfortunately, his taste in television will change. He will watch a steady diet of all-news channels and the Weather Channel. During viewing he will make remarks about the weather such as, "Holy shit, look at that blizzard, hurricane, mudslide, flood, and tornado!" And about the news, "Holy shit, what's wrong with people?"

Next month: Chapter 5—"What to Do about Those God-awful Clothes He Wears."

Baseball, Hot Dogs, Human Pie, and Chevrolet

Twenty-nine years ago my wife and I took our two sons to the Baseball Hall of Fame in Cooperstown, New York. The kids were eleven and nine at the time. This past summer the "boys" and I decided to take a road trip in my Chevy Malibu and revisit Cooperstown. My wife did not accompany us. It was probably a good choice.

Not that it was a terrible trip, but you have to understand that the boys and I are, to borrow a phrase from the TV series *MASH*, baseball perverts. We know things like Cumberland Posey's and Henry Manush's nicknames (Cum and Heinie). We know who holds the record for most putouts in games that were rained out between the fifth and eighth innings on Tuesday afternoons. (I won't spoil your fun trying to find the answer to that one.)

My wife would have to endure endless baseball talk. But she would be interested in knowing that other things haven't changed. For example, the boys still argue. During the first trip, one of their arguments might have gone like this:

Boy 1: Hey, guess what word is inside the word scope. (He was looking at a mouthwash bottle.)
Boy 2: Inside scope? Cope.
Boy 1: No, that's not it.
Boy 2: Yes it is.

Boy 1: No it's not. Cope is not inside the word. The *e* is at the
      end, not inside.
Boy 2: It's in the word, but it's not the word, so that's inside.
Boy 1: Inside, inside! Nothing on the ends. Don't you get it?
Boy 2: You're wrong.
Boy 1: You're stupid.

After that argument, anytime they had stupid disagreements, we would simply say cope-scope. They would get the hint and knock it off.

This time around the arguments were much more sophisticated and mature, matching their now advanced age.

Boy 1: Did you read that story about the pine tree at George
      Harrison's memorial? It was killed by beetles. How ironic
      is that!
Boy 2: It's not.
Boy 1: It's not what?
Boy 2: Ironic. It's just a coincidence, just like most of the stuff in
      that Alanis Morrissette song.
Boy 2: Of course it's ironic. Beetles killing a Beatles tree.
Boy 1: No. It just so happens that beetles killed the tree. Rain on
      your wedding day is a coincidence too. Morrissette had it
      all wrong.
Boy 2: So what's ironic?
Boy 1: The difference between what you expect to happen and
      what does happen. Like a Hollywood stuntman who re-
      tires and dies falling off a ladder while cleaning his gutters.
Boy 2: Well, I get the rain on your wedding day. You hope it
      doesn't rain, but you can't expect it not to. It might or it
      might not. But come on, beetles killing a Beatles tree?
Boy 1: Nope. Coincidence.

And on and on it went. Cope-Scope.

They still get hungry a lot too, but now they are adults. They are their own men. They can eat what they want when they want. So their, and sorry to say my, diet consisted of hot dogs, hot wings, hot peppers, hot fudge, hot onion dip, hot sausage, with hot sauce on almost all of them.

The effect of this diet was what you would expect. My daughter-in-law anticipated this and gave my son a can of Lysol with a note attached about its use on the long car ride. In the car at least we could open the windows. But windows don't open in hotel rooms anymore. Thank God we never came face to face with the poor lady who cleaned our room.

The worst, though, was that we spent a large portion of our time at the Hall of Fame Museum. On our last day's visit, right before we headed home, each of us got into a stall at the same time, doing our thing. It was our version of game of thrones. The music and the smell were bad enough, but all three of the toilets decided to have a bathroom malfunction. The sensors that trigger the flushing would not work...on any of them. (coincidence or irony?) The paper and the waste just sat there while the plaques of the hall of famers wished they could flip around and face the wall.

The malfunction wasn't our fault, but we did what all mature adult men would do; we just left. And as we walked away, we laughed like eleven- and nine-year-olds, which is close to the age of complete male maturation.

Next, I'd like to go back some day with my sons and grandsons. I just hope the toilets can handle us.

What, Me Worry?

Generally speaking, I am not a worrier, but sometimes I worry that I should be. Maybe there are some things that require more of an emotional response from me. Maybe if I worried about things, then I might be able to learn from them or prevent them from happening. Maybe worrying will force me to pay attention to the finer details of my life. So I ask you, dear reader of this fine publication (an unsolicited testimonial), should I worry?

Should I worry

- That when I take toilet paper off the roll, I have to make sure it is torn off exactly at the perforation, and, if it's not, I pick off the frayed edges?
- That my grandson has his toy cars up on blocks?
- When someone tells me I don't look so good, and I'm feeling my best?
- That every Saturday evening my wife gets all dressed up in a hot outfit and tells me she's going to church?
- That when I'm driving and come to a sign that says "Stay in your Lane," I can't decide which one I want?
- That I can't tell the difference between Selena Gomez's voice and Justin Bieber's?
- That my best friend truly believes that not only is President Obama the Antichrist, but he thinks the Pope is too?

- That because of global warming, ski slopes will have to be converted to water slides?
- About driving near people in Subarus because they seem to get into a lot of accidents, but they're the ones who survive?
- About not getting an early dinner reservation because sixteen thousand people turn sixty-five in this country every day?
- That my boomer friends drive little red convertibles, and I drive an old, gray Chevy Impala?
- That in song lyrics that have any form of the word *memory* in them, I enjoy replacing them with the word *mammary*?
- That families now spend mealtimes on their electronic devices instead of arguing and fighting like people used to do?
- That Hobby Lobby employees will be asking for raises because they'll have more mouths to feed?
- That the town in which I live has never made any lists of best places to live in the United States?
- That I've never eaten quinoa, kale, or hemp seeds, and probably never will?
- About lawsuits involving a bladder mesh, a pelvic sling, or transvaginal mesh? Should I worry that I don't know what they are, and that I'm afraid to find out?
- That the Catholic Church has only 250 exorcists?
- As a Chicago Bulls' fan, that LeBron James is still in the Eastern Conference?
- About Sarah Palin?
- That a new study reports that smelling farts could reduce the risk of cancer, strokes, heart attacks, arthritis, and dementia, and I have no sense of smell?

Let me know what you think, but if I don't hear from you, I'm not going to worry about it.

What if I Wrote This Article?

Did you read that book from last year called *What If?* Me neither, but what if I had some nonscientific answers to some absurd hypothetical questions? What if they were these?

What if manspreading on public transportation is deemed illegal? Surveillance cameras, similar to the red light ones, would automatically identify the spreader, and the city would fine the perpetrator $100. This would force men to sit with their legs together, crunching their reproductive organs and lowering their sperm count. This will make it more difficult for them to impregnate someone, resulting in the dwindling of the population, and therefore creating more room on public transportation that would then allow men to sit with their legs apart.

What if Elvis is still alive? All those suspicious minds are proven right when the eighty-year-old music icon is found living at the Heartbreak Hotel in Memphis with his hound dog and some hardheaded woman. All the fan mail sent there, however, is marked return to sender.

What if Chris Harrison, host of *The Bachelor* and *The Bachelorette*, had to get a real job? He eventually becomes a high school guidance counselor, but in later years he works as a florist where he sometimes tells customers, "This is the final rose."

What if the Chicago Cubs win the World Series? Immediately following the final out of the deciding game, the earth will stop spinning on its axis, trees, mountains, oceans, and small animals will fly out into space, and the earth will crash into the sun, or whatever the *What If* book says would happen if the earth stops spinning.

What if the things Dr. Oz tells us to use for weight loss, such as garcinia cambogia, green coffee bean extract, and raspberry ketone, actually worked? Nah.

What if it is discovered that secondhand vaping causes "cancer," an electronic type that attacks computers, cell phones, tablets, and so forth, and gradually erodes their memory? Eventually some geek genius invents a treatment for it called meme-o therapy.

What if Bob Dylan did a CD of opera arias? Look, he's already done a Christmas one. His most recent one is an album, if I may still use that word, of Sinatra covers. Why not old Bob warbling "FEEG a ROOOOOOW, FEEG a ROOOOOOW"? Critics will highly tout it because, well, because he's Bob fuckin' Dylan dammit.

What if Bitchy Resting Face was officially declared a disability? There would be PSAs done by Kristen Stewart and concerts given by Kanye West. It becomes a full-fledged charity, and telemarketers will call us, in effect, spreading the disease.

What if an episode of *Undercover Boss* featured the owner of a company, in a bad disguise, who goes into the trenches of his business? During his trench time, he finds out that he can't do any of the jobs. He learns that someone is not doing his or her job. He also discovers that, although he is making money hand over fist, his employees are struggling to make ends meet because they can't make a living on what the rich bastard pays them. At least one employee tells the UB that he'd like to send his kid to college but, of course, he cannot afford it because he is a single father with an infirmed parent living with him. Another one hasn't had a day off in five years, never mind a vacation. At the end, the boss fires the discontented employee, and gives a whopping $10,000 for the employee's college fund and the last employee $10,000 for a vacation. Everybody smiles, cries, and hugs at the end. OK, that *is* what happens on the show. But what if, off-camera, the person who got ten grand for school is pissed because he finds out what college really costs, while the vacation-money recipient takes his family of eight to Disney World for a week and still has to kick in $2,000 of his own money?

Jeb Bush will run for president, but what if, in order to deceive as many voters as possible, using the most common letters in the names of former presidents, he changes his name to Ira Noel. In an astounding move just before the election, President Obama, by executive order, sells Florida to Cuba, gives the money to bail out his home state of Illinois, and prevents Noel from becoming president, saving the country once again. If only.

A Man of Letters

Since I've become a huge celebrity, people are interested in contacting me. They want to get to know me more personally, hear my opinions, and ask for my advice. I cannot keep up enough with the tens, make that tons, of mail to answer them all. So I thought I would use this space to placate the masses.

Q. What do the initials in your name stand for, and why do you use them instead of your full name? Do you think it puts you on the same level as H. G. Wells, E. E. Cummings, and J. D. Salinger, or what? A. B. Normal, Normal, IL

A. I do it because I don't want readers to know that I'm a man. What's your excuse? By the way, currently I'm contributing more material than any of the slackers you mentioned.

Q. Where did you grow up? Adam S., Hollywood, CA

A. Nowhere yet.

Q. If you could only visit one place for the rest of your life, where would you go? William S., Enterprise, NV

A. To the bathroom.

Q. With your "talent" you can't possibly make a living as a writer. What else do you do? Mike R., Baltimore, MD

A. I taught junior high.

Q. Do you have any interesting stories? Arne D., Washington, D. C.

A. No, but I'll tell you this one. One eighth grade girl stopped after class. She said that a joke was going around that all the kids were laughing at, but she didn't get it. She asked, "If I tell you the joke, could you explain it to me?"
"I'll try. What's the joke?"
"What comes in quarts?"
"I don't know, what?"
"Elephants."
"Go home and ask your parents."

Q. You're a teacher. Maybe you can explain to me why people use "there's" with a plural, as in the sentence, "There's a lot of ways to make people laugh." Sandee B., Cleveland, OH

A. Well, you must understand that language is in a constant state of flux. People determine what eventually becomes proper usage. For example, many people now pronounce the *t* in often. It totally pisses me off, but that's language. In addition to language being very fluid, one must also keep in mind that there's a lot of stupid people out there.

Q. Where do you get your hair done? Christophe, Beverly Hills, CA

A. My hair was done a long time ago.

Q. When are you coming out with a book? Alfred K., New York, NY

A. The next time I leave the library.

Q. How would you summerize your philosophy of life? C. J. Parker, Los Angeles, CA

A. I would probably take it to the beach.

Q. Speaking of spelling, what do you think of language experts wanting to institute an International English Spelling Congress to invent a new system of spelling that makes more sense, fixing words such as cough and rough? Rosetta S., Arlington, VA

A. Although they may be determined, I think they have a tough job ahead of them. This change, however, will throw off all those National Spelling Bee contestants and the contests themselves. If the words are easier to spell, everybody could enter, and the Bees could go on for years. But I don't think there's much to worry about because any organization with the word Congress in it is not likely to get anything done.

Q. Which brings me to my question: in what political camp would you say you belong, liberal or conservative? Mitt R., Boston, MA

A. I don't like putting labels on my beliefs. However, there is a term that Yahoo commenters sometimes use for me when I give my opinions on news stories. They call me a Libtard, which I presume has something to do with me being a liberal who is not very punctual.

If I didn't get to your letter, consider yourself lucky.

The Funny Thing Is

My family doesn't think I'm funny. I don't understand it because I know they are totally wrong. And it's not just my word against theirs. I have definite proof. The proof is that *everybody* else in my life thinks I'm hilarious.

I taught junior high for more years than Illinois governors have been sentenced to serve in prison. During that stint, my reputation was that of a funny teacher. If a poll was taken, funny would have come in first ahead of boring and creepy.

Granted, the humor used to make twelve-year-olds laugh is not exactly *The New Yorker*. They have limited background and unusual sensibilities. For example, when trying to get more imagery in their writing, I might ask the students who have been on a roller coaster to explain to those who haven't what it's like.

Amid their suggestions, I might throw in: Eat about five tacos before you get on. Go on a coaster with a loop. When it reaches the top of the loop, throw up, which would really be throwing down. When the car gets to the bottom of the loop, be prepared to catch your lunch. This would always induce cackles, snorts, and, I'm sure, a little seepage in the pants. Trust me. They always lol'ed, no matter what grade, no matter what year.

With my friends, quick-wittedness outstrips cheap and arrogant. Case in point, my wife and I were at a party one night. We were all conversing and drinking when into the room walked a white cat with blue eyes. I like cats, so I put my hand down toward the cat and called him. It just continued walking. The hostess said that the cat was deaf. Without missing a beat, I began to use sign language. Instant, spontaneous guffaws.

At work, I was the guy who made people laugh most often and consistently. My colleagues would vote for humorous ahead of lazy and big-mouth know-it-all. Once again, an example: People had gathered in the teachers' lounge after school. On the table was a flyer from St. Paul Lutheran Church about some speaker that was appearing. In walked the girls' PE teacher who had been teaching a unit in health on sex education. She had in her hand a couple ex-tra handouts that were diagrams of the lower regions of a woman. When I walked in, I saw the church letterhead and the diagram, and I said, "What is this? St. Paul's letter to the Fallopians?" Uproarious reaction.

These are merely a few examples, but it is like that everywhere all the time. I do not say this to brag. I say it because I am perplexed as to why I am the funny guy in the real world but not around my family. No matter how witty, sardonic, or sophisticated my humor, the best I get is a half-smile and a head tilting backward.

I could blame it on the fact that all of them are humorless sour-pusses, but that's not true. They all laugh at whatever each other says. Even though one of their comments might be similar to some-thing I had said earlier, the other family member will get the laugh. I'm starting to believe it might be a conspiracy. One day they were all together when I wasn't with them. One of them got the idea and said, "No matter what he says, no one laugh." Someone else asked, "For how long?" And the answer was, "Forever."

Recently, much of the family was together. The conversation turned to travel. Someone mentioned that he had been to Clearwater, Florida, and saw the original Hooters that opened in 1983. I said, "How did it look, a little droopy?" Once again, the half-smile and head nodding backward.

During that same discussion, it was brought up that it was better not to stay with friends when traveling. It's because sometimes things are unsure. My nephew says, "You get up in the morning and wonder if there will be breakfast. Do they eat breakfast? Do we go out for breakfast? Do they at least have a Pop-Tart somewhere?" Huge laughs. Really? The Pop-Tart joke is better than the Hooters joke?

Maybe I should concede that my family is not my "room" and stop trying to be funny in front of them. Not that they would even notice the difference.

Deadline

I don't know how it is where you live, but my city newspaper lays out its celebrity obituaries next to those of, shall we say, more "ordinary" citizens. It's great that the columns for the regular Joes are about the same size as the celebs. It's the headlines that make the hoi polloi look bad. On one side the headline will say, *star of TV and movies* or *made important scientific discoveries.* Unfortunately, the other one dwarfs in comparison. It will say something like *loved family and career.*

That's nice, but that could be said of everybody. Well, OK, not everybody likes his or her job, and come to think of it, maybe everybody isn't enamored with his or her family. Regardless, my point is that these noncelebrities' obit headlines are too generic to summarize someone's entire life. They need some punching up.

So, as a public service, I created a list of more specific qualities and accomplishments to help with the process.

1) Walked up and down stairs until last day.
2) Achieved straight A's while homeschooled.
3) Could read 642 words per minute.
4) Rarely used the snooze button.
5) Didn't know who Ted Nugent was.
6) Always had three cats at a time, all named Fluffy.
7) Voted for Michael Dukakis.
8) Took to binge watching *House of Cards.*
9) Paid bills on time.

10) Looked forward to colonoscopies.
11) Sang well in the shower.
12) Always used a sponge to moisten envelopes.
13) Won the Pinewood Derby as a Cub Scout.
14) Still has highest score on Pac-Man at favorite bar.
15) Ate exactly 1,900 calories a day.
16) Loved palindromes, owned "*a Toyota.*"
17) Shared recipes with friends and never left out ingredients.
18) Could always tell the difference between Coke and Pepsi.
19) Watched the Weather Channel every day.
20) Had a two-year-old car with sixty-three miles on it.
21) Expert tiddlywinks player.
22) Made sweaters out of belly-button lint.
23) Never had a headache.
24) Once spoke the line "What Ho?" in community theater production of *Hamlet.*
25) Favorite "friend" was Chandler.
26) Apparently sent charitable donations to Nigeria.
27) Never missed Garbage Day.
28) Ate a handful of nuts every day.
29) Honest to the dentist about flossing.
30) Literally walked a mile in someone else's shoes.
31) Attended Disney World once, on its opening day.
32) Watched only G-Rated movies.
33) Still had Pet Rock collection.
34) Made career as fuzz blower in a box factory.
35) Asked for directions when lost.
36) Ate an egg fried on asphalt.
37) Kept ear and nose hair under control.
38) One of two people ever to appear on the *Newlywed Game* and *Divorce Court.*
39) Considered quirky, attended church every Tuesday.
40) Every week correctly guessed the killer on *CSI.*

My goal is to distribute this list to funeral directors across the country so they can help grieving families choose an appropriate headline with the cooperation of local newspapers. Can't find one that matches your loved one? Simply pick your favorite. I mean, who's really gonna know?

OAK SURGICAL INSTITUTE, LLC

Patient Rights and Responsibilities

III. Grievance Process

⋏ For any concerns you have while a patient with OAK SURGICAL INSTITUTE please contact our Executive Director at 815 928-9999 or through writing to Executive Director, OAK SURGICAL INSTITUTE, 403 South Kennedy Drive, Bradley Illinois 60915

Most grievances will be investigated and a written response will be sent within 14 working days.

⋏ You may also contact the Illinois Department of Professional Regulation (IDPH) without first filing a grievance with the facility. The address and phone number of IDPH is Illinois Department of Public Health, 525 west Jefferson, Springfield, Illinois, 62751 or phone 1-800-2528903, 1800-447-6404 (TTY), or Hotline 1-800-252-4343.

⋏ Medicare beneficiaries may also file a complaint or grievance with the Medicare Beneficiary Ombudsman. Visit the Ombudsman website at http://www.medicare.gov/ombudsman/resourees.asp or call 1-800-MEDICARE (633-4227) They ensure that Medicare Beneficiaries receive the help they need to understand Medicare options.

IV. Disclosure of physician financial interest or ownership

The following physicians have a financial interest or ownership in OAK SURGICAL INSTITUTE

⋏ Dr. Milton Smit

- Dr. Wesley Choy
- Dr. Alexander Michalow
- Dr. Michael Corcoran
- Dr. Rajeev Puri
- Dr. Eddie Jones
- Dr. Kermit Muhammad

The address for the above mentioned physicians is:

Oak Surgical Institute
403 South Kennedy Drive
Bradley, Illinois 60914

I. Policy on Advance Directives

It is our policy, regardless of the contents of any Advance Directive or instructions from a health care surrogate or attorney-in-fact, that if an adverse event occurs during your treatment at OSI, we will initiate resuscitative or other stabilizing measures and transfer you to an acute care hospital for further evaluation. At the acute care hospital, further treatments or withdrawal of treatment measures already begun will be ordered in accordance to your wishes, Advance Directives, or Healthcare Power of Attorney. Your agreement with this facility's policy will not revoke or invalidate any current health care directive or healthcare power of attorney.

We recognize and respect the rights of our patients. If you would like more information on Advance Directives please talk with a nurse in our facility.